GUIDE TO
MODERN BRITAIN

HAVE I GOT NEWS FOR YOU

GUIDE TO
MODERN
BRITAIN

Written by
NICK MARTIN

**HAT
TRICK**

**BBC
BOOKS**

Published in 2009 by BBC Books, an imprint of Ebury Publishing.
A Random House Group Company

Copyright © Hat Trick International Ltd 2009

Hat Trick International Ltd has asserted the right to be identified as the author of this Work
in accordance with the Copyright, Designs and Patents Act 1988

The Random House Group Limited Reg. No. 954009

Addresses for companies within the Random House Group can be found at
www.randomhouse.co.uk

A CIP catalogue record for this book is available from the British Library.

ISBN 978 1 846 07546 9

The Random House Group Limited supports the Forest Stewardship Council (FSC),
the leading international forest certification organisation. All our titles that are printed
on Greenpeace approved FSC certified paper carry the FSC logo. Our paper
procurement policy can be found at www.rbooks.co.uk/environment

Mixed Sources
Product group from well-managed
forests and other controlled sources
www.fsc.org Cert no. TT-COC-2139
© 1996 Forest Stewardship Council

Commissioning editor: Albert DePetrillo
Project editor: Laura Higginson
Copy-editor: Steve Tribe
Designer: O'Leary & Cooper
Production controller: Helen Everson

Printed and bound in England by Clays Ltd, St Ives plc

To buy books by your favourite authors and register for offers, visit www.rbooks.co.uk

CONTENTS

INTRODUCTION
BY IAN HISLOP

When the team at *Have I Got News for You* decided to produce a guide to Modern Britain, they could not have chosen a more suitable person to introduce it than myself. In many ways I embody the Britain of today and am about as cutting-edge, up-to-the-minute and hip-hop as you can get without actually being Lili Marleen. (*Lily Allen?* Ed.)

Viewers of the programme will know, for example, that I am famous for my stylish sense of dress and tend to wear an eclectic mix of suits and ties. Occasionally I overstep the mark, and my choice of a blue jacket with elbow patches in the last series was probably a mistake. Despite being assured that it was what all the young, trendy geography teachers are wearing nowadays, I think one can go too far in trying to follow fashion. After all, I am not Lilly Langtry. (*Lily Cole?* Ed.)

I am, though, a great fan of popular British music – or 'Britpop', as I believe the abbreviation has it – which is undoubtedly the best in the world and something that we can all share. My own favourites are Sir Edward Elgar, Ralph Vaughan Williams and Gustav Holst, but I am perfectly happy to listen to the more experimental sound of someone like Benjamin Britten.

And I must not forget my love of cinema. British Cinema is hugely respected and, like most Britons, I make a point of seeing all the very latest great films that have made it onto satellite TV. In the last month alone, I have seen *Zulu*, *In Which We Serve*, *Where Eagles Dare*, *Brief Encounter* and that marvellous epic about the *Titanic*. The black and white one with Kenneth More in it. *A Night To Remember*.

I could go on, showing just how closely my own taste matches current trends. 'Graphic novels'? I have just reread Mrs Gaskell's *North and South*, which is pretty graphic about the Industrial Revolution. 'Gaming'? I'm obsessed with Contract Bridge, and you can't drag me away from it. 'Social Networking Sites?' I have joined my local tennis club.

But now I am just 'twittering', as we call it, and the team were keen that I should not be overly immodest about the extent to which I embody the zeitgeist. So I will have to admit that the one area in which I am not entirely in sympathy with modern Britain is football. To be honest, I am not terribly keen on the game, although I gather that it is becoming more and more popular in this country, with a lot of people supporting clubs, going to matches and following the progress of their teams on television.

Fair enough, but I do not for a moment suppose this craze will last. It is certainly never going to be as popular as those mainstream obsessions which I share with the bulk of the population, such as reading, taking country walks, visiting old churches, going to art galleries and museums, and campaigning to restore the railway lines axed by Dr Beeching in 1963.

HOW TO USE THIS BOOK

This book is intended for the use of people who live in the United Kingdom (even those 6.3 million extra people living here who we don't know anything about). Since 2005, anyone coming to this country and intending to live here and become a citizen has had to show that they have knowledge of the English language and life in the UK. Indeed, since 2007, they have had to pass an examination in order to prove it. Until now, however, no book has ever been written specifically for those who happen to be living here *already*.

This is a curious omission, particularly given that a) there are many millions more of them, and b) let's face it, they probably have more disposable income available for, say, book-buying.

Also, given the tendencies of recent administrations, it could be that, in the future, not only will new arrivals be tested before being granted citizenship, but established residents could also find themselves having to sit some kind of examination, simply to continue living here. And this won't be like an A level. Oh, no. This'll be an exam some people might *fail*.

This is specifically *not* a 'User's Guide to the UK' – that title was rejected fairly early on, because of its unfortunate drug-related overtones. However, the Home Office publishes an official book entitled *Life in the United Kingdom – A Journey to Citizenship* (snappy, eh?), and this *Have I Got News for You* book should ideally be viewed as a companion to that. Or the antidote to that. Or, indeed, as nothing to do with that at all. Up to you, really. (Incidentally, when it was first published in 2004, the first edition of the Home Office's book became a runaway bestseller, so here's hoping.)

The Home Office book includes an invaluable 'Glossary of Key Words and Phrases', and it's intended that this book, too, will feature just such a section – not just because it may prove handy for the reader, but also because it'll turn out to be invaluable for filling up a few more pages when we've run out of ideas, and the publishers are getting heavy about deadlines and stuff.

Anyone buying the Home Office publication will notice that the preface to the 2007 edition features a photograph of the then Home Secretary John Reid, reprinted courtesy of the Department's official photographer:

Reid: Former Home Secretary

For the record, the photograph of Paul Merton that accompanies the preface to this book is reprinted courtesy of the Photo-Me booth on Hastings station.

Merton: About to catch a train

A revised edition of the Home Office's publication is somewhat overdue. Perhaps they've left the manuscript in a taxi, or something. Or perhaps they're just waiting to see whose photograph they should include alongside the preface. For once, their dithering has actually paid off – they must be so relieved that they hesitated, rather than going ahead while Jacqui Smith had the job. Otherwise the pulping mills would be working overtime (one of the country's few industries that would be).

Smith: Not really worth bothering to print her photograph in a book

PART ONE

THE MAKING OF
THE UNITED KINGDOM

WHAT IS 'THE UNITED KINGDOM'?

There is some confusion about the correct meanings and use of the terms 'United Kingdom', 'UK', 'British Isles', 'Great Britain', 'GB', 'Britain', 'British', 'Great British', 'England' and 'English'. Perhaps this diagram will help:

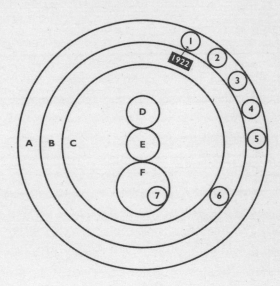

KEY:

A = THE BRITISH ISLES
1 = IRELAND
2 = JERSEY (OR GUERNSEY)
3 = GUERNSEY (OR JERSEY)
4 = THE CHANNEL ISLANDS
NO-ONE CAN EVER QUITE
REMEMBER THE NAMES OF
5 = THE ISLE OF MAN

6 = NORTHERN IRELAND
7 = THE ISLE OF WIGHT
B = THE UNITED KINGDOM
C = BRITAIN / GREAT BRITAIN
D = SCOTLAND (OR WALES)
E = WALES (OR SCOTLAND)
F = ENGLAND
1922 = 1922

Or perhaps not. Sometimes, the modern obsession with displaying information graphically can make things more confusing rather than less – as anyone who's watched news programmes on the BBC, ITV or Sky recently will already be aware (thanks to the throbbing headache, eyestrain, and nausea).

From this more than somewhat unnecessarily complicated diagram, we can see that, for example, the Isle of Wight (7) is within ring F, making it part of England, within ring C which means it's part of Great Britain, within ring B and therefore part of the United Kingdom, and within ring A thus forming part of the British Isles. Ireland, however, having been within ring B until 1922, then moved outwards to ring A, leaving Northern Ireland (6) within B.

As the diagram also illustrates, the Isle of Man and the Channel Islands, falling as they do *outside* ring B, are not part of the United Kingdom at all. Actually, their status is that of Crown Dependencies. You may well find this information stunningly dull, but that's exactly the sort of tedious fact people take great delight in testing you on.[*]

---

[*] *This is particularly true should you happen to enter a pub quiz anywhere in the UK. (Here's a good one – Who is the murder victim in Cluedo? Tricky one, eh? It's actually Dr Black.) In most other circumstances, this sort of knowledge is useless. Worse than useless, if we're being honest, because it's taking up valuable brain space that could be given over to something much more interesting and of more practical use. So the only thing to do is to apologise for ever having brought it up, and move on.*

You could, perhaps, now use the diagram as a board, and play some sort of weird game of darts instead.

The confusion over UK, GB, England, etc., is not necessarily a bad thing. It means that, whichever term a foreigner uses, a UK native is nearly always in a position to gently and, from the foreigner's point of view, irritatingly correct them. This will make the native English-speaker feel cosily superior, if only for a minute, and can help enrage the person they're talking to. Here's how it works...

A Spanish acquaintance, who speaks English fluently, is telling you how they go to the beach at least four times every day, adding, 'Of course, the weather at home means I can do that – not like here in England.' Politely suggesting 'Here in *Britain...*' in a voice that is only just audible should put them nicely off their stride. If they then nod and say, 'Thank you... "not like here in Britain",' the next step is to murmur, 'You probably mean *the UK*, actually.' This will normally bring the conversation to a natural end.

The concept of 'Britishness' is a difficult one to define. To paraphrase an old saying: 'Some are born British; some achieve Britishness; and some, like Madonna, have Britishness thrust upon them.' (Which makes Guy Richie a much braver man than most of us.)

So, officially, four countries make up the United Kingdom – England, Scotland, Wales and Northern Ireland. England and Scotland are 'Kingdoms', Northern Ireland is a 'Province' and Wales is described as a 'Principality'. Amongst other things.

A question often asked is this: Legally and constitutionally speaking, what is the difference between a 'Kingdom', a 'Province' and a 'Principality'? A good question, and exactly the sort of query that Google was invented for.

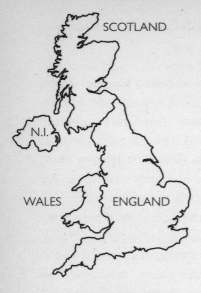

MAP OF UK

MAP OF UK BASED ON POPULATION

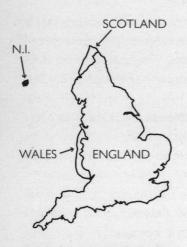

MAP OF UK BASED ON PROJECTED RISE IN SEA LEVELS (luckily)

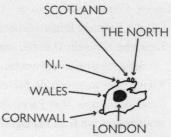

MAP OF UK BASED ON OWNERSHIP OF TASTEFUL CARPETS

NATIONAL CHARACTERISTICS

ENGLAND

The English are often accused of arrogance by their United Kingdom brother nations. This is rather unfair, as the English people who live in places like Cornwall or Somerset or Lincolnshire or Northumberland aren't like that at all. It's really only those smug London and Home Counties bastards who get on everyone else's nerves. Basically, the sort of people who speak and behave like Jonathan Ross. But not *actually* him, you understand.

When it comes to the UK's population, the English, of course, enjoy a huge numerical superiority. Take this analogy – if the UK is a typical high street, then Northern Ireland is an awkwardly placed fruit stall, Wales is a damp, odd-smelling charity shop, Scotland is a steel-shuttered off-licence, and England is a chain of overpriced coffee shops. Which it more or less is, anyway.

SCOTLAND

The Scots are a fiercely independent people – is anyone ever *mildly* independent? – and proud of their history. Centuries of being treated really rather badly by the English came to an end when Tony Blair came to power, and Scottish people began to fill nearly every post in the Cabinet. Today, some of the most influential people in the UK are Scottish: Prime Minister Gordon Brown, Chancellor of the Exchequer Alistair Darling, and Lorraine Kelly.

Scottish people are prominent in all walks of life, although having said that, you do see considerably less of Billy Connolly these days, now that Parkinson isn't on any more. Makes you wonder how we'll all manage without those jolly and surprisingly frequent updates on what the Big Yin's been up to.

In the past, the Scots have always had a reputation for, and prided themselves on, their ability to handle money – witness the prudent example of, among others, Scrooge McDuck.

The Scottish financial sector was a source of considerable national pride for some 200 years – in fact, right up until Sir Fred Goodwin came along and ballsed it up completely by running the Royal Bank of Scotland into the ground. Sir Fred stepped down from the company in October 2008, and to show their utter disapproval of his role in bringing down one of the country's great banking institutions, the RBS board granted him a pension of just £14,000 a week.

The Royal Family make much of their Scottish connections. Whenever male members cross the border into Scotland, they always make sure to have a selection of kilts at the ready, so that the minute they emerge from the train or plane they can quickly change into one, and pass unnoticed amongst the locals. The degree to which they manage to look comfortable wearing them varies, as can be seen in these photographs from the Royal archives. (It helps to remember that these kilts are being worn in a country that is cold, windy, and covered in thistles. By English people. Well, more or less English.)

Guess where these pictures were taken?

The Royal Family are keen to make a point of spending what the rest of the country calls 'the summer' at their Scottish estate, Balmoral. The property was bought by Queen Victoria – her estate agent was very amused – and it was she who started the tradition of going there every year and forcing the rest of the family to stay with her. Contemporary accounts make clear what sort of person she was, so the surroundings and prevailing weather conditions will doubtless have suited her temperament perfectly, the old bat.

When in Scotland, the Royal Family are careful never to miss the various annual 'Highland Games' competitions, often being photographed grimly attempting to have a good time despite a) the rain, b) the midges, and c) the presence of large men with beards trying to up-end trees and throw big stones for no discernible reason.

Big stone: Just bung it over there, Jimmy

Tossing the caber: Easier than moving a tree. But not much

WALES

Famous Welsh people include Dylan Thomas, Neil Kinnock, Max Boyce and Huw Edwards. When not too busy doing the whole Scottish thing, the Royal Family also make a point of playing up their Welsh associations. The Prince of Wales is, in fact, as the name suggests, not just any old Prince, but a Prince of *Wales* – so there. It's a very important difference, apparently. Well, important to the Welsh. Or is it the English?

Princes William and Harry are, by tradition, Princes of Wales as well. They even go so far as to use 'Wales' as their surname, which is a bit odd, given that their surname is actually Windsor. Although technically, of course, their real surname is Saxe-Coburg-Gotha, the 'dynastic' name having only been changed (for fairly obvious reasons) during the First World War. In some ways, it's a shame, as the original one is a much better name for comedy purposes: that whole *they're all really Germans, anyway* thing always gets a laugh. Having said that, it is probably just as well that the family surname isn't still Saxe-Coburg-Gotha, seeing how, in the armed forces, they like to display your name on a label above the ciggie pocket of your shirt.

**Saxe-Coburg-Gotha: A less convenient surname
if you're going to wear it on your shirt**

However, it's worth remembering that since Prince Phillip was born a member of the house of Schleswig-Holstein-Sonderburg-Glücksburg, then theoretically so was his son, Prince Charles, and so were his grandsons, William and Harry. Good luck with that one. Schleswig-Holstein-Sonderburg-Glücksburg – it sounds like the name of Germany's top advertising agency.

W. SCHLESWIG-HOLSTEIN-SONDERBURG-GLUCKSBURG

Even trickier:
Schleswig-Holstein-Sonderburg-Glucksburg

The Welsh are often fiercely protective of their national identity. In 2001, the botox-faced TV presenter and journalist Anne Robinson, when being interviewed by Paul Merton on the programme *Room 101*, remarked that she didn't like the Welsh, describing them as 'irritating and annoying', and adding: 'They are always so pleased with themselves.' This provoked a furious backlash in Wales against Ms Robinson, who, it should be pointed out, has never in her life shown the least sign of being irritating, annoying or pleased with herself.

NATIONAL IDENTITY IN SPORT

Sport is one of the areas where national identity seems to be ever more important and yet the situation is becoming increasingly confused. There are four 'national' teams for England, Scotland, Wales and Northern Ireland in football, and this gives rise to much friendly rivalry between the individual nations. Whenever England are playing an international match, the Scots always pretend they're going to support the other side - for example, they 'joke' that they would even cheer for the 'Robert Mugabe All Stars' if England happened to play against them in some competition or other. English supporters always laugh good-naturedly at that sort of joshing, and hardly ever let it irritate the hell out of them.

In many other sports, however, the country fields a United Kingdom team, although we enter a 'Great Britain' team at the Olympics. This team has come to be referred to as 'Team GB', an idea that in no way smacks of a rather desperate and massively uncool PR branding exercise. And it's not even an accurate term, as it should technically have been called 'Team GB&NI' (see earlier confusing diagram).

The use of these terms depends entirely on context; if a Welsh hurdler in Team GB wins a medal, he's the triumphant Brit – if he loses, he's the unlucky Welshman. If an English sprinter wins, she stays English – if she loses, she's the plucky British also-ran.

All in all, the issue of nationhood in UK sport is a bit of a mess, frankly, but no one's ever going to do anything about it, so there we are. It's only bloody sport anyway.

Famous people from Northern Ireland include the late George Best, Gloria Hunniford and that bloke who used to be in *Cold Feet*. Oh, you know – the one that did the *Yellow Pages* ads for a while. Yes, you do. Your mum likes him.

Northern Irelanders have their own unique way of speaking – for example, to English ears, the sentence 'How now, brown cow' comes out sounding like 'Hoy noy, broyn coy'. But that's OyK.

They also say 'whenever', when they really mean 'when'. No one knows what they say when they mean 'whenever'. And they tend to tack the phrase 'so he did' or a similar linguistic 'tag' onto the end of sentences, as in: 'He went mad, so he did.' The purpose behind doing this has never been entirely clear and, when challenged, they claim to be completely unaware of doing it, so they do.

A SHORT HISTORY OF THE UNITED KINGDOM

BRITAIN IN PRE-HISTORY

Palaeontology tells us that modern man (Homo sapiens) arrived in what is now Britain some time before the last Ice Age. It would have been earlier, but there was the wrong sort of ice on the line. Because the sea level was a great deal lower, the land mass was joined to the Continent, so it was relatively easy for humans to settle here by simply walking across, and large numbers appear to have done so – being strongly encouraged to keep moving on by the French.

Fortunately, at that stage of human development there was no real concept of 'jobs' as such, so the problem of one group within a society complaining loudly about an influx of people from elsewhere coming over here and taking them was a long way off – it would be many centuries before the evolution of 'Homo Kelvinmackensis'.

In due course, however, with an Ice Age on the way, the temperature started dropping, and the early settlers began to leave. For a long time, campaigners had been proposing Europe-wide action on measures that might have prevented this 'global freezing', as it was known, but there had been a notable lack of consensus and no coherent agreement on the way forward.

One of the suggested approaches was that the polluter should pay, but there were a number of difficulties with this. The world's largest methane producers at the time (the mammoths, and not, as you might think, the French) felt they were being unfairly penalised and staged a walk-out, effectively bringing that particular round of negotiations to a halt. Especially as they'd walked out, quite literally, over everyone else.

Around 12,000 BC, Britain was repopulated as the climate warmed up again, a process that still occurs every August bank holiday, on a much smaller scale. When the ice began to melt and the waters rose, Britain was separated first from Ireland (a separation that had fairly far-reaching political consequences down through the centuries), and then from the rest of continental Europe, creating the so-called 'Garlic Gap'. The present-day configuration settled down some time around 6000 BC.

Before the Romans arrived, there appear to have been regular links between the residents of the island of Britain and those of the Continent already. The Continentals were keen to foster semi-permanent trade links in order to maintain a regular supply of the commodity for which Cornwall has always been famous. Sadly, the pasty market collapsed around 550 BC, largely as a result of the Continental invention of the 'calzone', so the disappointed Cornish traders were forced to switch to dealing in tin instead. Indeed, in the *Histories* of the Greek writer Herodotus, the British Isles are referred to as the 'Tin Islands'. (The original manuscript of his works, however, shows that he originally labelled them the 'Pasty Islands', but this was crossed out and corrected in another hand – presumably that of his rather more up-to-date editor. How the cuisine of Rome itself might have been affected, one can only speculate. Similarly, one wonders why the people of Cornwall never hit on the idea of combining their two greatest assets by coming up with the tinned pasty.)

Pasty: Market collapsed

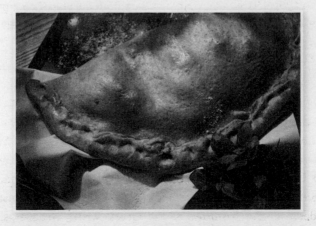

Calzone: Startlingly similar

'WITH EUROPE, BUT NOT OF IT.'

In the century before the Romans invaded, Britain had seen successive waves of immigrants from the Continent. Many of them were, in fact, fleeing the Romans, and found themselves displaced as the Empire grew. Perhaps it's not too implausible to suggest that Britain's reputation as a safe haven for refugees and dissidents dates back as far as this. And it's also possible to speculate that the lingering resistance to attempts to bring Britain into line with any larger political body already well established in the rest of Europe can be traced back this far, too – it surely can't just be a coincidence that the issue of our relations with the European Union is still such a political hot potato today.

In the relatively recent past Britain's relationship with Europe has divided whole political parties to an extent that sometimes damages their electoral prospects, as happened to the Conservatives. In addition, the UK staunchly defends its decision not to sign up to the Schengen Agreement, which abolished border posts between the participating countries on the mainland, and which makes it possible to drive from southern Spain all the way up to Finland's border with Russia without ever having to show a passport. Except when booking into a hotel. Or changing money. Or paying a speeding fine. Or trying to get yourself released from prison, assuming that your passport and every item of identification you own weren't confiscated earlier along with all your other possessions including your shoelaces and belt, before you were led sobbing into a damp cell that smells of other people's urine and fear. But perhaps that sort of thing doesn't happen any more.

Unfortunately, SATS tests hadn't been invented, so it's obviously almost impossible to assess with any degree of accuracy the level of literacy in the Ancient British Isles. It seems fairly clear, however, that Ancient Britons weren't really bothered about writing stuff down; if any of them tried, none of it has survived. We all know how difficult it is sometimes to find a pen – imagine how much harder it must have been with only eight pens in the entire country. So it's the Romans who appear to have brought writing with them when they invaded in AD 43. They were, naturally, keen record-keepers, because records are always useful if you're attempting to run an empire or keep control of a population, as the Nazis discovered some nineteen centuries later.*

So it is with the arrival of the Romans that we start to know rather more about what was going on. Not that this early information is always terribly accurate, dependable or trustworthy – Julius Caesar himself highlighted the problem at the time, when he famously said, 'Veni, vidi, wiki' ('I came, I saw, I was given some error-strewn unreliable nonsense').

We know about Boadicea mostly thanks to the Roman senator and historian Tacitus. Boadicea (now apparently to be known as Boudicca, or Boudica – a bit like how you're not supposed to say

---

* Seen in a historical context, CCTV and databases are, after all, only the latest means by which those with a controlling instinct have attempted to monitor the activities of those they would control. The Romans would probably have used them if they'd been invented, and would undoubtedly have found them useful. If nothing else, when all those slaves stood up and started claiming to be Spartacus, the bloke in the surveillance chariot could have radioed through saying, 'OK, Sarge, we think we've got a match – it's the bloke at the front who looks a bit like Kirk Douglas.'

Bombay or Peking any more) was Queen of the Iceni tribe who rebelled against Roman rule, and she had considerable success for a while in thwarting their plans and generally being an irritant. This made her something of an inspirational figure in the British psyche: thwarting the plans of others and generally being an irritant has served us well as key elements of Britain's relations with foreign powers for many centuries.

Boadicea: Irritated Romans with constant spelling changes

The fact that she was a woman and yet succeeded, for a while at least, in running rings round the Roman army must have irritated the Hades out of the swarthy mummy's boys from Latium. She overran and sacked the towns of Colchester and St Albans – curious targets, one might think, but then there weren't all that many decent-sized settlements to trash if you wanted to make a political or tactical point. ('Come on, chaps – surely we can come up with somewhere a bit more exciting than St Albans to overrun... Anybody? Oh well, it'll have to do, I suppose. But she's not going to be pleased.') She did also destroy Londinium, but that was, if anything, even less of a headline-grabber, given that it was a small, relatively new Roman garrison town – think of it as a first-century Aldershot. Without the glamour.

Boadicea was eventually defeated in the somewhat prosaic-sounding Battle of Watling Street. Watling Street was one of the many long, straight roads the Romans are so famous for having constructed and maintained. According to some, this is evidence of their civilising influence, but others see road-building as merely another of the means by which oppressors have traditionally maintained the upper hand, since it enables the more efficient deployment of troops. Hitler was able to claim that all he was doing was creating jobs and investing in infrastructure right up to the moment the tanks started to roll smoothly along the autobahns in the direction of one neighbouring country or another.

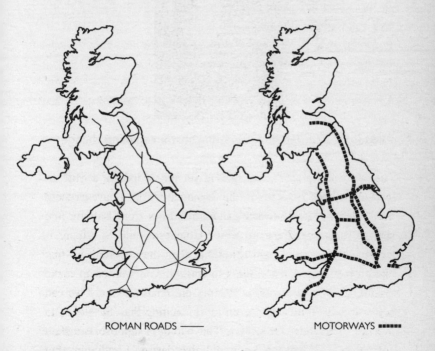

ROMAN ROADS ——————   MOTORWAYS ▪▪▪▪▪▪

There were approximately 2,000 miles of well-maintained roads in Roman Britain. There are approximately 2,000 miles of motorway in Britain today. Can this really be just a coincidence? Yes.

As is well known, the Romans appear to have decided that the effort of conquering Scotland was just too great for the material rewards on offer. After all, North Sea Oil wouldn't be discovered and come on stream for at least another 1,900 years, and the benefits of the versatile and peculiarly Scottish culinary technique which has come to be known as 'deep-frying' were at that stage unfamiliar to them. Meanwhile, the Emperor Hadrian arrived on an official visit to Britain in AD 122 ('Hello – and what do you do? Oh, you're a legionary, are you – well done, keep up the good work. Hello – and what do you do? Oh, you're a legionary, are you...'). It was as a result of the Emperor's desire to buttress the borders of the Empire that Hadrian's Wall came to be built. 'Hadrian's Wall': not the most imaginative of names perhaps, but the tendency to give boring names to building projects is well documented even in more recent times ('We really have to settle on a name for that white house you're going to be living in, Mr President.' 'What shall we call this new bridge we're building across Sydney harbour?' 'Who left this slice of gherkin on the plans for my new office block?').

Construction of Hadrian's Wall was finished within six years, the original estimate having been three, although, to be fair, they did keep altering the spec from one week to the next as the project progressed. This is nearly always a recipe for arguments, overruns, overspends and general friction between the project manager and the contractors, as anyone who's seen Kevin McCloud on Channel 4 every week for the past few years will already know. Incidentally, if *Grand Designs* had been around in Roman times, McCloud would doubtless have been unable to resist declaring at some point (usually just before the second ad break) that his big worry is that Hadrian and Vibia are going to be unable to maintain the integrity of the project in key areas of the build.

**Hadrian and Vibia: Were they able to maintain
the integrity of the project in key areas of the build?**

The finished wall ran for some seventy miles right the way across northern England, the route taken lying just below the current border with Scotland.* It's estimated that, in the periods of greatest unrest, it would have been garrisoned by something approaching ten thousand men. This would have been good for the local economy, for example providing work for anything up to ten Ancient British prostitutes – they earned their money in those days. Hadrian's Wall is reckoned to have been one of the most heavily fortified frontiers of the entire Roman Empire – quite a distinction, but bear in mind it had to keep out people who were *Scottish*.

And while it seems pretty impressive to have built a Wall this big, the task does rather pale into insignificance alongside the later Great Re-Pointing project of AD 327.

It is perhaps worth remembering that work on the Great Wall of China began some 600 years earlier in the fifth century BC. In its most extensive incarnation it ran for more than 4,000 miles rather than seventy-odd, and it is estimated, at its peak, to have been guarded by somewhere in the region of a million men. Knowing that, one can't help feeling Hadrian's effort was, by comparison, a teeny bit half-hearted. You'd have thought a wall down the middle of the British Isles from top to bottom would have been a natural progression, but somehow the Romans always had more important things to be getting on with. Orgies, generally.

ARTHUR, KING OF THE BRITONS

With the departure of the Romans in the early fifth century AD, the history of Britain becomes swathed in the mists of myth, as Chris Eubank wouldn't – or more accurately couldn't – say. Various small kingdoms rose and fell; Angles and Saxons began to arrive. While the Saxons were quite a learned people, the Angles were much less educated – everyone's heard of obtuse Angles. And as for the Jutes, it's not really worth discussing a race that considered it acceptable to name themselves after a kind of sacking (that's the fabric kind of sacking, and not the kind that Boadicea did earlier to Colchester and St Albans). It's doubtful that it's even possible to talk of there being such a thing as 'Britain' in any meaningful sense at this stage. In reality, there was a collection of various tribes who cohabited peacefully or warred with each other on a fairly regular and, to the modern mind, fairly random basis. No one quite knows to what degree the tribes would even have been able to communicate with each other – an inhabitant of Cornwall might have had as much chance of understanding what a resident of Northumberland was saying as a Geordie would have of understanding, say Brian Sewell (i.e. a really small chance, same as the rest of us).

The biggest individual name to have hit the headlines in this period was King Arthur, although, of course, there's no real proof that he ever really existed. Newspapers didn't exist either, so there wouldn't have been any headlines for him to hit. Despite this, Arthur remains in many ways a national hero and symbol, and has survived through the ages by being immortalised in significant works of art, such as Mallory's *Morte d'Arthur* in the fifteenth century, Tennyson's *Idylls of the King* and the paintings of Burne-Jones in the nineteenth, and Monty Python's *Monty Python and the Holy Grail* in the twentieth. (Although one has to make allowances for the deeply unsatisfactory and massively disappointing ending of that film – plainly, they ran out of either ideas or money or both. And just wait until you see what effect similar constraints have had on the ending of this book. Not to mention the beginning. And the less said about the middle, the better.)

The Round Table: Historians believe the perspective may be a bit out, and that in reality King Arthur probably sat round the edge

Arthur is, of course, most famous for his Round Table, the first British monarch to achieve renown on the basis of their furniture (although it is fair to say that Edmund the Magnificent owes his epithet at least in part to having invented the folding deckchair during the long hot summer of 942). Arthur is also credited with the invention of a radical new seating plan for tables, which did away with the outmoded notion of 'boy-girl-boy-girl-boy-girl', and ushered in the ground-breaking concept of 'boy-boy-boy-boy-boy-king'.

In theory, every one of Arthur's knights seated round the table was of equal status, an idea which seems to appeal on some deep level to modern sensibilities. In practice, of course, too much democratic accountability has been viewed as an impertinence by leaders in the modern age. So the British Prime Minister (unlike other despots) by tradition chooses never to sit at the head of the Cabinet table, but rather in the middle of one side in order to emphasise the collective nature of Cabinet decisions (and also to have first go at the plate of biscuits). But let no one be under any illusion: prime ministers usually manage to get their way in the end. A variety of techniques to achieve this have been employed by the various holders of the office to greater or lesser effect: completely dominating the conversation and the agenda; staging a sudden internal leadership election to silence critics; threatening a Cabinet reshuffle, or simply reshuffling out of a job those who regularly express their disagreement; offering private meetings outside Cabinet and making members *think* their opinions are valued, before going right ahead and doing what they were always going to do anyway; sulking for weeks on end until they get their way; etc.

Quite how democratic Arthur's court (if it ever existed) with its Round Table (if *that* ever existed) can have been is therefore open to question. The modern Prime Minister has a Cabinet of perhaps twenty-five members; according to some versions of the Arthurian legend there were about 150 knights knocking around Camelot during Arthur's time. Getting a policy agreement from all 150 of them would have been like trying to nail jelly to the wall. Incidentally, Mallory lists some more obscure knights, and along with Sir Launcelot and Sir Galahad can be found thoroughly top-notch chaps with thumping good names like 'Sir Belliance Le Orgulous'. Rather more poetic than simply being called First Secretary of State – coincidentally, a title currently held by Lord Mandelson Le Oleaginous.

Mandelson: Oleaginous

But as a potent symbol of whatever it is that is Britishness, King Arthur has lived on in the imagination of the British as no other figure has. One of the many legends surrounding the King has it that, in the hour of the country's greatest peril, Arthur and his knights will rise once again and come to our defence. Some people find it comforting to believe that might be true. Although perhaps less comforting is the realisation that, if it is true, the reason Arthur hasn't arisen can only be that the hour of the country's greatest peril hasn't arrived yet. Oh dear.

VIKINGS

The word 'Viking' comes from the Old Norse word *vikingr*, so it hasn't come very far, having dropped only one letter on its journey into modern English. Vikings were sea-going Scandinavian warriors, explorers and traders who struck out across Europe over a period of about 200 years from the eighth century. They're known to have travelled as far east as Istanbul and as far west as Newfoundland, so they got around a bit.

Curiously, whilst the public image of the Vikings has been undeniably shaped by the fact that they are almost always depicted in drawings or in films as wearing horned helmets, there is, in fact, no proof whatsoever that they ever did so. Just as there is no proof whatsoever that the former Cabinet minister David Mellor wore a Chelsea strip whilst conducting his adulterous affair in the 1990s with an 'actress' who had appeared in some 'artistic' films. Yet Mellor's public image was undeniably shaped by his association in the minds of the public with a particular item of clothing. Whilst many people remember the image of a Viking in a horned helmet, it's reasonable to assume that most people have forgotten the image of a rather sad, middle-aged lothario Secretary of State shagging an actress while dressed only in his pants and a Chelsea shirt. Unless, of course, somebody thoughtlessly dredges the whole sorry business up again more than seventeen years later in, say, a book. It's not fair on either the Vikings or Mellor really, but there we are. Still, at least Max Clifford wasn't involved in publicising that whole horned helmet business. So far as we know.

Vikings: Almost certainly didn't wear helmets like this

Mellor: Almost certainly didn't wear Chelsea strip

Apart from the helmet, one of the things with which the Vikings are principally associated in people's minds is *Danegeld*. Although sounding very much like a member of a 90s boy-band, Danegeld is actually a form of tax. Danegeld is possibly the only one in history more unpopular than the 'Poll Tax' (which was itself introduced, coincidentally, by the Thatcher government in which the selfsame David Mellor served as a minister).

The first occasion on which, it is thought, Danegeld was handed over was when the Vikings attacked Paris in the ninth century. The attackers were effectively bribed to lay off by the payment of a large amount of silver and gold. However, it would surely be unfair to draw any conclusions from the fact that it was the French who gave the Vikings the idea, prepared as they were to hand over a vast amount of money rather than fight. Indeed, should the phrase 'cheese-eating surrender monkeys' have sprung into the minds of any readers, it surely did so unbidden. Danegeld was not so much a tax as an early form of protection racket. ('Nice country you've got here, Æthelred – wouldn't want to see anything happen to it, know what I mean?')

A few years after this genius scheme had been piloted in Paris, King Æthelred handed over a big wodge to buy the Vikings off and prevent further attacks in England. Realising they were onto a good thing, the Vikings were back within a few years, turning up outside London and demanding money with menaces. This pattern continued, although the Vikings (unlike the Inland Revenue who are entitled to twice-yearly payments on account from anyone who's self-employed, and whose reminder letter regularly turns up within two days of the end of the tax year) at least appear to have submitted their tax demands only once every five years or thereabouts. One curious result of the large sums of money being fleeced from the indigenous population and repeatedly shipped abroad is that more Anglo-Saxon pennies have turned up in Scandinavia than have ever been unearthed in Britain. A similar phenomenon will probably come to light when future archaeologists in Brussels excavate the area surrounding the headquarters of the European Union.

WILLIAM THE CONQUEROR

Interestingly, the Normans too were descended from Vikings ('Norsemen') who had settled in northern France in the early tenth century. The fiefdom of Normandy came into existence under King Rollo, who turns out not just to have been a character created for an animated children's TV programme. (And if you allow Tony Benn as the inspiration for 'Mr Benn', then *he* really existed, too. Although there's no evidence that anyone called 'Crystal Tipps' has ever walked the Earth.)

Rollo: Real

Benn: Real

Tipps: Not real

William the Conqueror was also known as 'William the Bastard'. As epithets go, 'the Bastard' at least sounds a bit hard. A good test of the macho quality of such soubriquets is to imagine them being used by a darts player: 'Ladies and Gentlemen, will you kindly give a warm Lakeside welcome to the reigning British Darts Champion – Andy 'The Bastard' Webster.' It's hard to imagine the epithet 'The Bald' ever making it onto the back of a darts shirt: on the whole, the Holy Roman Emperor Charles II can consider himself pretty unlucky to have got stuck with that particular one.

As every schoolboy knows, William's invasion of England took place in the year 1066. So ingrained is this number in the British consciousness, incidentally, that if you ever find yourself stuck outside a building with a keypad entry system, it's got to be worth giving it a go. Failing that, give 1966 a bash. It's bound to be one or the other.

1066: Got to be worth a go

Having become King, it is said that within four years William had succeeded in eliminating the English aristocracy and supplanting it entirely with people who were personally loyal to him. A remarkably similar exercise was carried out by Tony Blair when he came to power, although it only took him about half as long to pull it off. And he didn't need any heavy cavalry or archers, just people like Peter Mandelson. So, much more deadly, then.*

Attempting to express the impact of the Norman invasion in modern newspaper-speak may help to give the *Guardian*-reader, accustomed to such terminology, some idea of the astonishing scale of their achievements. The Normans effectively embarked upon a process if not of ethnic-cleansing, then at the very least of the ethnic stratification of the already relatively stratified society to guarantee the continuance of the financial and cultural disadvantage of the Anglo-Saxon underclass by such means as dominating the built environment, the creation of a national government database, the reform of the legal system by the overwriting of centuries of custom and practice and the imposition of another culture and language on the indigenous population.

Oh, and as if that wasn't enough, they were quite happy to run through with a sword anyone who disagreed with them. It was the original hostile takeover, and nothing in Britain would ever be the same again.

---

* *It is quite well known that before a law can be entered onto the statute books of the United Kingdom, it has to receive the Royal Assent – the express agreement of the Queen or King, although in modern times this has tended to be a mere formality. What is possibly less widely known is that this assent is still, somewhat surprisingly, expressed in the manner and language of the eleventh-century French invaders. Once a piece of legislation has gone through all the necessary stages in both the Commons and the Lords, it is then returned to the Lords and presented to the Clerk of the Parliaments. In the absence of the Monarch, it falls to the Clerk to signify the royal assent, which is done in the traditional French way: a prolonged but lethargic shrug accompanied by the uttering of the word 'Bof'.*

THE CRUSADES

The Crusades were a series of military campaigns waged by Christians against Muslims. (It's advisable to say that to avoid being blown up.) Because of its association with these campaigns, the word has acquired significant cross-cultural baggage. When George W. Bush used 'crusade' in a reference to the conduct of his 'war on terror' in a speech televised live to the entire world a few days after September 11th, it was one of two things: it was either deliberate (i.e. ill-advised) or accidental (i.e. stupid). Deciding which is what's known as a 'no-brainer'. As, indeed, is he.

Bush: Trying to choose between one of two things

The First Crusade began in the 1090s, and the Ninth in the 1270s, so the term 'Crusades' actually covers battles, sieges and miscellaneous fighting conducted in the Middle East over a period of nearly two hundred years. (If nothing else, by the twentieth century, conflicts in the region had scaled down considerably in terms of duration: the Yom Kippur War of 1973 only went on for about twenty days, and the 'Six Day War' of 1967 lasted, well, six. There's progress for you.)

Ostensibly, the reason for launching the Crusades was to recapture the Holy Land, more specifically Jerusalem, from the hands of the infidel hordes. Once again, the words used in this connection are charged with political and religious significance. To the Christians, the Muslims were infidels, whereas to the Muslims the Christians were, um, infidels. So, had both Fox News and Al Jazeera existed at the time, their reports, delivered from opposing standpoints but inevitably using the same terminology, would have been exact mirror images of each other. Even down to the direction in which their news ticker-tape captions moved.

It's ironic, given the prevailing tensions between the supposedly Christian West and the Islamic world, that successive popes declared that anyone who went off on a Crusade and managed to get himself killed would automatically have his sins forgiven. No matter how serious his offences in his life up to that point, anyone dying in a Crusade would thus go straight to heaven. So there you go – the Crusaders were not that much different from the suicide bombers who go to their deaths with the promise of being tended by 72 virgins in paradise ringing in their ears. But then again, the Crusades took place 800 years ago and, while the popes have moved on a little bit since then, some imams are still shipping out suicide bombers on a regular basis. So come on guys, meet us halfway, eh?

Richard I (also known as 'Richard the Lionheart' – now there's a darts-player epithet if ever there was one) is the King most associated with the Crusades, at least in the minds of the British public. And by that, we mean the 3.4 per cent of the British public who actually know what the Crusades were. By all accounts, he spoke English with a heavy accent, and spent very little time in the land of his birth – he's estimated to have been here for only six months during his ten-year reign, complaining that it was always cold and raining. So, a sort of medieval Sean Connery. But none of this prevented him becoming a bit of a cult figure, if not at the time, then certainly after his death, and a statue of him mounted on a horse and brandishing his sword stands outside the Houses of Parliament today. Not only a proud symbol of royal heroism, but also a desperately unimaginative backdrop for countless TV news interviews with MPs.

Statue of Richard I:
'My lisht of complaintsh now includesh pigeonsh.'

Richard was described as very good-looking, with blond hair and pale eyes. He's also said to have had a very close relationship with his mother, and to have been particularly fond of writing poetry in French. However, it's not certain whether he was also a keen fan of musical theatre and soft furnishings.

MAGNA CARTA

Much significance has always been placed on Magna Carta. Issued in 1215, it has been described as a turning point in the relations between subjects and sovereign. King John, who succeeded his brother Richard I, was forced by his barons to accept the provisions it set out. This story of a man forced to deal with tangled affairs in the absence of his brother was also the inspiration for the iconic 1970s Michael Caine film, *Get Carta*.

Magna Carta proclaimed and enshrined in law certain rights and responsibilities, and forced the King to accept explicitly that he too was bound by the law. Unless, of course, he was ever caught speeding, in which case we'll say no more about it, Your Majesty.

Some of the provisions introduced by Magna Carta are more relevant today than others. Reading clause 33, for example, we can see that the rebellious barons turn out to have succeeded in their demands for the removal of all fish weirs (a victory no doubt claimed by Ye Super Soaraway Sunne to have been brought about by their sustained campaign on behalf of the British fishing industry). However, one of the main provisions, and the one to which reference is always made, is that of the 'Writ of Habeas Corpus' – the right of a court to demand that any person being imprisoned be brought before it in order for it to establish whether the detention is lawful or not. A fundamental principle in both English and American Law for nearly eight hundred years, *habeas corpus* nevertheless proved far too inconvenient for the Bush administration when it came to Guantanamo Bay. So they simply ignored it. And in the UK the Government has repeatedly tried over the last few years to increase the length of time the police are able to hold someone without charge – an issue which many see as an attack on the fundamental principles of Magna Carta. But hey – everything will go back to the way it was after the war on terror has been won, won't it? Whenever that is. Don't hold your breath – unless, of course, you're being waterboarded by the CIA.

Below are two photographs of the Magna Carta – one is of the original document, and the other is of a copy. Years of painstaking research by scholars have finally established which is which.

Although it seems pretty obvious once you know: the real one is portrait, the copy is landscape. Derr.

THE TUDORS

The year 1485 saw the arrival on the scene of the Tudors, a dynasty that included such near-legendary figures as Henry VIII, Elizabeth I and Lady Jane Grey, who claimed the throne for just nine days in 1553, but was executed for her pains in early 1554.

Henry VIII of course, as everyone knows, was married six times, and the fascination with his wives never seems to go away.

Professor David Starkey has claimed, however, that the emphasis on his marital affairs is down to the feminisation of history in the modern age by female historians, and that undue concentration on Henry's love life prevents people from focusing on the political consequences of his reign. Be that as it may, for him to have contracted six marriages is quite exceptional – particularly when one thinks of the hassle that Prince Charles received over his plans to marry Camilla, having also succeeded in getting rid of his previous wife. By divorcing her, obviously. No other implication was intended.

Henry it was who broke away from Rome and branched out on his own as head of the Church of England. A bit like Robbie Williams and Take That. Although in the case of the Church of England and the Catholic Church it's harder to say which one has ultimately had the more successful solo career. Just as with Robbie and the boys, however, there are frequent rumours of an impending rapprochement, although it's fair to say in both cases that the chances of them getting back together again in any meaningful way are pretty slim. Unlike Gary himself. Or Robbie come to that.

Prior to creating the Church of England (to be headed by himself) and getting himself excommunicated, Henry had had the title *Fidei Defensor* – usually translated as 'Defender of the Faith' – bestowed upon him by none other than the Pope. This title is still used by the monarch, and today it appears on coins as 'Fid. Def.' (coincidentally, also what Puff Daddy is currently calling himself).

Prince Charles has, however, let it be known that, given the multicultural, multidenominational, multifaceted religious nature of British society today, he would prefer to be known as 'Defender of Faith'. (Who's she? Another mistress?) A neat linguistic shimmy by HRH, there: hair-splitting in Latin is clearly just the thing to bring the monarchy into the twenty-first century.

Queen Elizabeth I was the last of the Tudor monarchs. Despite being the daughter of Anne Boleyn, Elizabeth managed to avoid the benefits of having an extra finger and a supernumerary nipple; little things that set her mother apart during piano lessons and in the changing rooms at school.*

THE CIVIL WAR

The term 'Civil War' has come to refer to a series of wars and political struggles that took place between 1642 and 1651. At issue was who ultimately held power in the land, which involved the not exactly small matter of the right and ability of the citizens (or at least the gentry) to hold the King and his ministers to account through their duly-appointed representatives in Parliament.

King Charles I tended to regard Parliament as an irritating and irrelevant inconvenience, and tried to avoid getting involved, or indeed summoning one, for as long as he could get away with it. He believed absolutely that he was ordained by God to govern the country in any way he saw fit and to appoint whichever ministers or advisers he felt necessary, and he was disdainful of Parliament's attempts to force him to justify his actions and hold him to account. He felt that questioning or scrutinising his actions and the actions of the ministers he had appointed was an affront. In effect, he really only bothered with Parliament at all when he absolutely had to, and that was generally only when he needed to impose taxes or fight a war, for which he required the consent of Parliament. During his time in power he also turned a blind eye both to the fact that people accused of crimes were regularly imprisoned by his allies without due legal process being observed and without the right to

---

* NB there is no actual proof that Anne Boleyn had either of these unusual characteristics, but it's another of those factoids that's right up there with David Mellor's Chelsea strip – everyone knows that it's probably not true, but passes it on to others as a fact, simply because it's more fun to treat it as if it were.

challenge testimony, and to the fact that it was becoming common practice for testimony and confessions extracted through the use of torture to be held to be admissible.

Should any of this sound familiar, and were any readers tempted to draw parallels between the attitude and behaviour of King Charles I and that of any modern Prime Minister – perhaps particularly in relation to the general disdain for Parliament, the turning of a blind eye to people being imprisoned by his allies (in a detention centre in Cuba) without due legal process, and to the fact that it was becoming common practice for testimony and confessions extracted through the use of torture to be held as admissible – they are, of course, at liberty to do so.

However, it was not Charles I's destiny to end up schlepping himself around on the international 'rubber-chicken' lecture circuit being paid $250,000 a throw, and raking in an estimated £12 million in the first eighteen months after leaving office. Instead, as everybody knows, his fate was slightly less humiliating: his head was chopped off in a London street.

The beheading took place in Whitehall right outside the Banqueting Hall, only about two minutes' walk from Downing Street. After a general election, eager soon-to-be Prime Ministers drive over the very spot on their way back from Buckingham Palace, ironically enough after having been invited to form a government by Charles I's rather more polite and democratically enlightened successor.

So, after the Civil War and the very un-British spectacle of a regicide, came a brief period when the country was a republic under Oliver Cromwell, who assumed the title of Lord Protector. Cromwell remains a controversial figure to this day, but it is surely a measure of his place in history that, nearly 350 years after his death, he managed to make it into the BBC's poll of the *100 Greatest Britons*, and in a creditable tenth place, too. That's just two places below John Lennon.*

It is, however, something of a tragedy that whilst Oliver Cromwell presumably said lots of interesting things during his life, the only quote anyone seems to remember is the one where he urged a portrait painter to paint him 'warts and all'.

Cromwell: Spot the wart

---

* *And to allow readers to judge the validity of this important and well-respected survey, it's worth mentioning that, despite polling strongly, Queen Victoria ended up being nudged into 18th place. By Michael Crawford, who came in at number 17. Yes, that Michael Crawford.*

It's rather bad luck if, despite having been a significant political leader and living a life as full of incident as he did, the best-known thing about you is that you had warts. A suitable parallel would be if the only thing anyone could ever remember about Iain Duncan Smith was... Nope, sorry, it's gone.*

Oliver Cromwell represented the constituency of Huntingdon in Parliament, but nobody else remotely interesting has ever held the seat. From 1979 to 2001, for example, the MP was John Major.

THE VICTORIANS

The Victorian era, as a certain well-known online encyclopaedia informs us, is named after Queen Victoria (no citation needed, apparently). Thank God for online encyclopaedias, eh? Otherwise, we'd all still be thinking it was named after the railway station. Or the type of plum. Or perhaps even the sponge cake. It also reveals that the Victorian era was preceded by the Georgian era, and succeeded by the Edwardian era, though it neglects, on this occasion, to tell us after whom those particular eras are named. So, unfortunately, we're none the wiser. Still, that's Vicipedia for you.

---

* *On the subject of memorable quotes, Paul Merton once pointed out on an episode of HIGNFY the difficulty of making sure your 'famous last words' are worth writing down for posterity. As he explained, the real problem is that, having come up with something particularly pithy and memorable, you then have to just shut up. Whatever the temptation, it's essential to keep shtum until your actual demise. It's no good delivering yourself of some weighty opinion about the state of the world, or a profound reflection on the very nature of existence, and then blowing your dignified place in the reference books by adding, 'Tell you what, though, I could murder a cheese sandwich . . . aaargh.'*

Victoria's real first name was Alexandrina. She realised very early on, however, that an historical period called the 'Alexandrinian era' was likely to be an unpopular one given the difficulty of saying it in the first place, so she wisely went with her second name. She was the granddaughter of George III and the niece of William IV, quite a reasonable CV for a monarch. Also, in those days, being almost entirely German was pretty much a prerequisite for a king or queen of this country, and she comfortably ticked that box as well. Jawohl! – Alles in Ordnung!

A rare, 'off-duty' photograph of Queen Victoria.
At a car boot sale, apparently

Victoria became Queen in June 1837 on the death of her uncle, William IV, who had no surviving legitimate children. (More bungling by London's social services. Heads should have rolled.) William did, however, manage to produce ten illegitimate ones with his mistress, who was (not surprisingly, given the tradition that male royals should always shag actresses) an actress.

William IV's fathering of so many illegitimate children appeared to cause barely a raised eyebrow in royal circles, but times had changed, and rule by a monarch who rejoiced in the epithet 'the Bastard' (see above) was no longer deemed viable. When it came to the succession, it was to William's nearest legitimate relative that the finger of fate duly pointed. Tradition tells us that at the age of 10, on learning of her probable destiny during a history lesson, Victoria declared, 'I will be good.' She didn't actually specify at what, but one of the things she turned out to be spectacularly good at was getting pregnant. She married the German Prince Albert of Saxe-Coburg and Gotha (where the dynastic name came from – see above), after proposing to him in October 1839. It sounds a bit forward of her – it wasn't even a leap year – but in fact it was all down to royal protocol, what with her being monarch and all. (Although it must have sounded a bit odd if she proposed using the royal 'we': 'Albert, will you marry us?' Makes her sound rather working class and Northern. And who's to say if she even went down on one knee? She was pretty short to start with, and anything could have been happening under that big dress.)

In total, she and Albert had nine children, and Victoria was pregnant on and off for a period of about seventeen years. Ahhh, bless: that means she must have loved babies, doesn't it? Unfortunately, no it doesn't. Her letters and diaries subsequently revealed that, in fact, she absolutely loathed being pregnant, hated giving birth, found babies utterly unappealing, and frankly didn't have much time for children in general anyway. All of which perhaps goes some way towards explaining Victoria's renowned air of unamused-ness.

It's well known that Victoria had an astonishingly long reign: 63 years, 216 days. By way of comparison, were Prince Charles to come to the throne on 1 January 2010, pledging to beat his illustrious great-great-great-grandmother's record, he'd have to carry on kinging until 4 August 2073, by which time he'd be 124 years old. Just imagine how many of those jolly-expensive-but-really-rather-more-ish shortbread biscuits he will have shifted by then.

AN AMUSING MYTH?

The catch-phrase with which Victoria is most associated is, of course, 'We are not amused.' But it's by no means certain that she ever actually said it. As catchphrases go, it's not one of the snappiest, it has to be said, but it has certainly stood the test of time. Brucie, had he been asked, would probably have said, 'We are not amused – amused, we are not.' And bearing in mind that, by the time she came to the throne, he was already topping the bill at the Palladium, it's surprising he wasn't even consulted.

Victoria's children married into many of the royal families of Europe – this, she believed, would help stabilise Europe and guarantee cordial relations between the countries in the future ('cordial relations' being the Victorian term for 'happy families'). Yeah, well, nice try, but sadly misguided seeing as the First World War broke out less than fourteen years after her death. Mind you, the thoroughness of the job she did in marrying her children off to the crowned heads of Europe is evidenced by the fact that, for example, the Queen, Prince Philip, King Juan Carlos of Spain, Queen Sofia of Spain and ex-King Constantine of Greece are all great-great-grandchildren of Victoria and are therefore all cousins. Not so much a case of 'chinless wonders' as 'chinless – and no wonder'. The effect of Europe's royal houses keeping their gene-pool the size of a puddle can also be seen in the faces of three of her grandchildren, first cousins Tsar Nicholas, George V and Kaiser Wilhelm. The resemblance between them is startling – certainly a great deal closer than the resemblance today between Anne Robinson and, say, the Anne Robinson of ten years ago.

Facial hair forecast:
Russia (Tsar Nicholas II) – beardy.
Great Britain (King George V) – beardy

Germany (Kaiser Wilhelm): Moustachey at first...

... but with outbreaks of beard later.
Also in later years he ditched the whole
'skull-and-crossbones hat thing' as being 'far too 14–18'

A few years later, the style was reinvented by the Nazis after they had succeeded in reviving the whole 'world war thing'

The Victorians were very, very good at some things. Engineering was something they really cracked, and one of its manifestations was the flourishing of the railways from about 1840. This was despite a few hiccups in the early days: during the inaugural journey of the Liverpool and Manchester railway some ten years earlier, William Huskisson, a popular MP (and yes, amazingly, in those days there was such a thing), became the first person – or at least the first famous person, and therefore worth writing about in *The Times* – to succeed in getting himself run over by a train. It's a funny thing, but, one way and another, someone being killed at a launch party can often put a bit of a dampener on proceedings, and it was certainly not really the sort of headline the L&M's PR company had been hoping for on the next day's front pages.[*]

What appears to have happened, according to contemporary reports, is that when the train came to a halt for a while during the outward leg from Liverpool, Huskisson spotted the Duke of Wellington, who had come along for the ride, and he left his carriage to say hello and have a chat. (Well, you would, wouldn't you?) Unfortunately, he was promptly flattened by a hitherto-unnoticed

---

[*] *Or rather, as front pages were, at the time, the back pages. The front pages of nineteenth-century newspapers carried nothing but a mass of microscopically small advertisements – comparable to the average internet page nowadays.*

Stephenson's *Rocket*. You have to concede that, given that there were probably only about fifteen railway engines in existence in the entire world at the time, Huskisson certainly had grounds for considering himself pretty bloody unlucky.* (Although spare a thought for the other passengers, whose onward journey was severely delayed, owing to what an L&M spokesman could only describe as 'the wrong kind of MP on the line'.)

**Stephenson's Rocket: Difficult not to notice it
steaming towards one, one would have thought**

---

* *Frank Skinner has an interesting theory regarding the circumstances surrounding this fatality. Skinner speculates that the Duke may actually have been trying to warn his companion about the approaching* Rocket, *but Wellington was known to have had a very early set of ill-fitting false teeth... Tragically the name 'Huskisson' is probably not the easiest name to have to shout out if one has wobbly dentures. Huskisson may well have been in the very act of cupping his ear and saying, 'Sorry, Your Grace, didn't quite catch—' when he got a* Rocket *up his backside, so to speak.*

In fact, as the day wore on, things didn't really improve for the Iron Duke: when he and his party finally arrived in Manchester they were jeered and pelted with bricks, a traditional local welcome for any visiting la-di-da southerner, then as now.

The Stockton and Darlington Railway was the first permanent steam-powered railway line, opening in 1825. (Engineers carefully planned every last detail of the route, making absolutely sure it avoided running through the nearby hell-hole hamlet of Middlesbrough.) Stockton and Darlington seem like two rather unpromising destinations from the point of view of passenger numbers, but the choice of route was down to the fact that the line would link several collieries to the port of Stockton, so it seemed like a jolly good idea at the time. Interestingly, when it opened the Stockton and Darlington Railway merely owned the tracks. It didn't operate the trains; other companies paid fees for the right to run trains along the line. Nor do the trains appear to have run to a coherent timetable in any sense. They tended to operate somewhat haphazardly, with services running at the whim of the operating companies, who would send out trains whenever it suited them.[*]

....

....

Industrialisation continued apace throughout the Victorian era, together with the expansion of the Empire, and the height of men's hats, as the supreme self-confidence of the age carried the Victorians and their way of life ever further out into the world. It takes a fair degree of self-belief to feel comfortable with and indeed rejoice in a title like 'Empress of India', as Victoria did from 1876 onwards, and the Victorians seem to have had it in spades. Everything they did, they approached with a virtually bullet-proof sense of their own worth: from architecture (the

---

[*] *The dotted lines above have been left blank for readers to fill in their own respectful homage to the 'no-change-there-then' tagline so beloved of the writers of jokes for topical news quizzes on radio and television over the last twenty years or so.*

Houses of Parliament, Manchester Town Hall, New Delhi) to massive civil-engineering projects (Brunel's bridges and tunnels, Bazalgette's sewers) to museums and exhibitions (the Great Exhibition of 1851, Crystal Palace), to dizzyingly high headgear (the Topper, the Stovepipe, the Even Bigger Stovepipe and the That's-Not-A-Hat-That's-A-Roll-Of-Linoleum.)

If the Victorians were confident of their place in history, they were pretty sure of their role in the world too. This they saw as, well, basically getting to boss Johnny Foreigner around most of the time – for his own good, mind, because left to his own devices look what a mess he made of running the show, eh? Christianity, science, the British legal system, afternoon tea, dressing for dinner, and a well-nigh total ignorance of foreign culture – the Victorians took all these with them whenever and wherever they ventured abroad. Sometimes, of course, they encountered resistance to the whole idea from Johnny Foreigner in person, which could lead to a certain amount of administrative inconvenience or other forms of unpleasantness. To counteract this, the Victorians took the pragmatic approach of both speaking loudly *and* carrying a big stick. This 'stick' – generally in the more effective form of vastly superior firepower – was wielded more often than not in defence of the Empire, and many a native rebellion was put down in a fairly loudly spoken, big-stick-carrying manner over the years.

It appears to have taken several generations for that characteristically Victorian mindset (i.e. the fundamental belief that everything would be absolutely fine if everyone else would basically shut up and do whatever Britain says) to wear off. Indeed, some would say its pervading influence is discernible in Mrs Thatcher's famous and repeated 'handbagging' of our European Union partners during negotiations in the 1980s. Today, the country's dealings with the rest of the world seem to be characterised by two qualities: 1) a vaguely uncomfortable, guilt-ridden post-imperial clumsiness, and 2) a somewhat hesitant diffidence arising from the difficulty of figuring out what 'being British' actually means. Such national self-doubt would no doubt have been completely incomprehensible to the robust Victorian mind. As would wearing a hat less than four feet high, or spotting an amused Queen.

Queen Victoria lived to see the dawn of the new century. She died in 1901, which was very considerate of her: had she died a year earlier, pub-quiz pedants up and down the country would have been able to drone on endlessly about how it's really rather fascinating but a common misconception is that Queen Victoria lived to see the dawn of the twentieth century, when technically of course, she did nothing of the sort, because the new century didn't in fact begin on 01/01/1900 but on 01/01/1901... zzzz...

THE TWENTIETH CENTURY

What can one say about the twentieth century that hasn't already been said before? Well, lots of things, probably, for example: 'The twentieth century had the shape and overall texture of a kiwi fruit' – which may be complete drivel, but it's never been said before. But it is clearly not easy to attempt to sum up a century as fast-paced and turbulent as the twentieth in a few paragraphs, and get some jokes in as well, so be nice.

In the 1970s and 1980s, the most important events of the twentieth century would often be neatly distilled into a single memorable phrase, chorused whenever England played Germany at football: 'Two World Wars and one World Cup, doo-dah, doo-dah.'* In truth the build-up to and the aftermath of the two world wars totally dominated the historical skyline as far as the UK was concerned: England's victorious 1966 World Cup campaign

---

* 'No World Wars and no World Cup' was, of course, the corresponding chant on the terraces in Switzerland.

arguably presented fewer historically significant repercussions by comparison.

Despite the fact that the rulers of the major European powers were all direct descendents of Victoria (see above), it seemed like no time at all before Europe was embroiled in the biggest conflict the world had ever seen. It was going to be the 'war to end all wars', though sadly it didn't, and in 1939 it all kicked off again. To put this brief gap between the two world wars in perspective, think of it this way: had Episode 1 of the first series of *Have I Got News for You* been transmitted on the day of the signing of the Treaty of Versailles, the Second World War would be due to break out right in the middle of Series 40, in December 2010. Which would be unfortunate – if only because, every week, you'd end up having to do the same story for the first footage question in Round One. ('Well, it's the Second World War again, isn't it, Kirsty?')

An early example of the classic panel-show seating plan: President Wilson and the US delegation at the Versailles conference

And so to round two

BRITAIN TAKES FLIGHT

Three years into the century (oh, all right, two then) the first flight took place in the USA, when the Wright Brothers succeeded in getting the first heavier-than-air device off the ground. It's a much-repeated fact that, at 120 feet, the total length of their pioneering flight was less than the total length of a Boeing 747.

After the developments in America, Britain really joined the aviation era properly in 1909 when Louis Bleriot undertook the first cross-Channel flight, taking off from a field somewhere near Calais and landing just outside Dover. Sure enough, he was soon listing the route on his website as 'Paris (Calais Plage) to London (Dover Cliff)'. And, at 37 minutes, his pioneering flight lasted longer than a programme made for an American 'one-hour' TV slot.

To some degree, the loss of an Empire and the search for a new role in the world was the story of Britain in the twentieth century. As the years went by, however, various roles suggested themselves and, to a certain extent, at different times Britain now plays all of them, either consecutively or simultaneously, on the international stage. Within Europe, Britain plays the role of foot-dragging, thorn-in-the-side, opt-out fanatic. In relation to the Commonwealth: avuncular if slightly awkward club president. And when it comes to America, Britain often plays the role of cheer-leader, bezzy-mate and confidant, thanks to what came to be referred to by the British as the Special Relationship, and by the Americans as 'Huh?'* In fact, since the Second World War, US Presidents have always made a point of maintaining at least reasonable relations with their British counterparts, just in case they need them to provide a fig leaf of international respectability when they're planning a war: 'Hey, I know what – get the Brits on board somehow and we can say we're not acting unilaterally, we're building an international coalition.' It usually works – at least, it always worked with Blair.

And how did the twentieth century end for Britain? Oh. With the Dome. They say there's nothing like ending on a high, and that was indeed nothing like ending on a high.

---

* *In fact, during Gordon Brown's first visit to Washington following Barack Obama's election in 2009, some commentators were quick to point out that the term the new US administration were using was not 'Special Relationship' but 'Special Partnership'. It's hard to judge precisely what the implications of this shift of terminology might be. If someone says they've formed a 'partnership' with someone else, that could mean pretty much anything. However, if someone maintains they're in a 'relationship' with someone, everyone else assumes they're shagging. That's certainly what some commentators believed the relationship between Tony Blair and George W. Bush was all about – metaphorically speaking, of course. And it was always fairly plain who got to be on top.*

PART TWO

HOW BRITISH SOCIETY HAS CHANGED

IMMIGRATION

From Angles and Jutes to Poles and Bulgarians, there is a long tradition of immigrants coming over here, taking the jobs British people can't be arsed to do. Many people living in the UK today can trace their origins back to other countries – in Europe, the Middle East, Africa, Asia and the Caribbean. In the distant past, waves of invaders came and stayed for one reason or another, although it's safe to say it's unlikely to have been for the weather. Or, until the first Chinese takeaway opened in 1958, for the food.

Britain has always been proud of its tradition of offering a place of refuge for people who are escaping war, prejudice and hardship, from the French Protestant Huguenots in the 1700s, who fled from religious persecution, and the Irish in the 1840s, who fled from the potato famine, to the Ugandan Asians in the 1970s, who fled from the regime of Idi Amin, and the Poles in the 2000s, who fled from compulsory mullet haircuts and stonewashed denim.

In the past few years, however, with large numbers of economic refugees making their way across Europe and hoping to settle in Britain, the welcome has been somewhat less enthusiastic. In essence, the UK's more recent efforts have boiled down to:

1) helping to coordinate the large reception centres built outside Calais
2) deciding to close those same centres down
3) reinforcing the alarmed fences around our Channel Tunnel terminal, and
4) hoping the French will deal with the problem at their end.

Which, from time to time, they do – by clearing the temporary, unofficial camps which are being squatted in by the people who would have been in the reception centres, if they hadn't all been closed down. All rather unsatisfactory for everyone concerned but, since it's not actually happening at our end of the tunnel, it only makes the news sporadically so British politicians only have to think about it very occasionally, which suits them just fine.

1980s TO PRESENT

Home Office statistics show that in the 1980s, somewhat surprisingly, it was the USA, Australia, South Africa and New Zealand that provided the largest immigrant groups to the UK. In the early 1990s, it was people from the former Soviet Union who began coming to Britain in search of a new life. They integrated well, finding jobs and buying up football clubs and spending their own hard-earned [*Check this, please*. Ed.] money on new players in such a way that, soon, no other clubs could compete with them (unless they happened to find themselves a spare sheikh to help out around the place).

In the final years of the last century, and the early years of this one, it was the Poles who kept Ryanair busy, as the promise of well-paid jobs in the UK lured them to these shores in sizeable numbers. Many of them found work quite easily and, as EU citizens, they had the absolute right to remain in the UK. Since there was a distinct shortage of plumbers over here, the Poles filled the gap. (And, while Nature abhors a vacuum, a Polish cleaner certainly doesn't.) One unexpected consequence of this influx was that it provided UK joke-writers on topical comedy news quizzes with a convenient source of Pole-based material for several years. Particularly with regard to things like pre-Election *'polls'* – do you see? (*Surely better than that?* Ed.)

However, as the downturn in the UK economy began to bite in 2008, the Poles started going home in considerable numbers. This was undeniably a blow to the writers, and in turn led to some of them having to seek alternative work – some are even known to have taken on so-called 'dirty' jobs, such as writing links for Bruce Forsyth on *Strictly Come Dancing*. It's easy to see just how inter-related the countries of the EU are, if even something as unlikely as the quality of Brucie's links can be affected, for better or worse, by the migration habits of Eastern Europeans … Eastern Europeans, the migration habits… of!

CASE STUDY: THE GURKHAS

One group campaigning in 2009 for their right to settle in this country were the Gurkhas. In 2008, the Government lost a case in the High Court and was forced to start backing down on its previous restrictions on allowing the Nepalese soldiers to settle in Britain, the judgment stating that the country's 'debt of honour' should be acknowledged.

But once the initial media bandwagon had moved on, it emerged that, rather sneakily, a significant amount of small print had been attached to the reviewed proposals, in effect significantly reducing the numbers of Gurkhas qualifying for residency under the new measures.

What happened next displayed British democracy in microcosm. There was, as it turned out, a genuine groundswell of support for the Gurkhas among the general public. In 2009, this was combined with an uncomfortable feeling that the Government hadn't quite played fair over the whole business. Imagine that. So when the Liberal Democrats forced a vote in the House of Commons in May 2009, the MPs who inflicted an embarrassing defeat on the Government were, in many ways, only reflecting the opinion of the public in their constituencies (an all-too rare occurrence in itself, the cynic would say).

The Gurkhas were able to bring in a whole army of socio-economic statistics on their side of the argument, but nothing counted quite so heavily in their favour as the involvement of a beautiful and rather posh actress to plead their cause. Since the very early days of the campaign, the Gurkhas had enlisted the help of the fragrant yet formidable Joanna Lumley to act as the 'public face' of the issue – Lumley's father had served alongside the Gurkhas, and her commitment to their cause has been unwavering.

Joanna Lumley struck the fatal blow against the Government when she manoeuvred the hapless Immigration Minister, Phil Woolas, into an impromptu but very public meeting. She appeared to get him to agree to several of her requests there and then, on camera, making it look like Government policy was being made and remade on the hoof, or rather on the high heels.

One can't help thinking that at least a few slightly confused members of the public were saying to themselves, 'Gosh, this thing with the Gurkhas must be pretty serious – even that mad Patsy woman has sobered up and got her act together to help them.'

This is probably the best example of celebrity campaigning since Jimmy Savile endorsed the seat belt.

Lumley: On a higher level than Woolas.
In more ways than one

Obviously, there's nothing wrong with well-known people using their fame to highlight issues and causes that they believe in – look, for instance, at the way Jim Davidson has ceaselessly championed pig-ignorant intolerance. For anyone who has to put up with the considerable inconveniences of being famous in the modern age, trying to use your fame to achieve something worthwhile might well be some sort of consolation. But it's not hard to imagine that many equally worthy issues and causes are routinely ignored as a result of being unable, or unwilling, to play by the rules that today's media always seems to want to play by. The lesson from this is clear: Got an issue? Get Lumleyed up. And always remember the Gurkhas' war cry – 'Ayo Gorkhali!' ('Oh, piss off, Gordon!')

THE CHANGING ROLE OF WOMEN

From Joanna Lumley to Kerry Katona, from Katie Price to Dame Stella Rimington, from Shami Chakrabarti to, well, take your pick of any of the gobby ones on *Loose Women* – it's clear the role of women in UK society today is changing. For instance, it's hard to believe but, until 1882, when a woman married, her money, earnings and property all automatically became the property of her husband. The situation as regards the family, divorce, employment, and so on, is now very different for women, though the law is far from perfect in many people's eyes.

Here's an entirely hypothetical example: suppose a fabulously-wealthy-but-apparently-rather-naive former member of an internationally famous 1960s beat-combo with National Treasure status, was persuaded to marry, say, an ambitious but not-in-any-way-wealthy former model from the North East of England who lost a leg in a traffic accident, and have a child fairly soon afterwards. And suppose the relationship was almost inevitably to founder on the grounds that, as would have been blindingly obvious to just about everyone else in the entire world, they had absolutely nothing whatsoever in common apart from, oh, let's see, the initial letter of their surname. In such a case, the courts today would be entitled to take into account the desire of the former model to carry on living the multi-millionaire lifestyle to which she has become accustomed, and award the ambitious-but-not-in-any-way-wealthy former wife a suitable financial settlement to enable her to do so. Society has certainly come a long way in that respect.

According to Government figures, in Britain today women make up fifty-one per cent of the population. Given this statistic, it's curious that only about ten per cent of the people in online chat rooms who say they are women *are* women. No one quite knows why this should be. Well, maybe they do, but they're not saying, and frankly the whole business sounds slightly unsavoury, so let's move on.

Women also account for about forty-five per cent of the workforce. There are now more women than men at universities and, on average, girls tend to leave school with better qualifications than boys – to be honest, it's not looking good, is it, chaps?*

In the past, traditional areas of employment for women were healthcare, secretarial work, retail work and teaching, but there is plenty of evidence that women today are active in many more areas than ever before. Although not all: in the field of comedy, for example, one has only to look at the number of times Jo Brand is obliged to appear on *QI* to be able to come up with a realistic assessment of the inroads made by women into that particular area.

One readily observable consequence of there being more women than ever before going out to work, is that many of them appear to be under the impression that it's perfectly OK to do their make-up while on public transport. (Were this the letters page of the Daily Telegraph, *there would now follow several days' worth of correspondence on the subject 'Dressing Tables: Whatever Happened To Them?') Having to watch someone apply their morning make-up on the Tube can be really annoying for those sitting opposite, who never quite know how to react. What is often particularly effective is feigning total disinterest during the process but, once they've finished, doing a huge, overly-theatrical double-take and announcing loudly to the entire carriage, 'Blimey – who'd have thought a bit of cheap slap could make such a massive difference, eh, lads?'*

Home Office research shows that, nowadays, 'very few people' believe that women should not go out to work and stay at home instead. 'Very few people' can be taken in this context to mean... well, this man, basically:

Housework, however, is one area where women continue to shoulder the lion's share of the burden, although there is some evidence that men are gradually taking more responsibility for such matters. Some men even go so far as to place their empty pizza boxes in the bin in the kitchen, rather than just tucking them under the sofa and concealing them behind that flap of material that hangs down at the front, whatever it's called.

In childcare, too, which was long regarded as primarily 'women's work', British fathers are increasingly coming to share the task of looking after their own children. This consists almost entirely of taking them to McDonalds on the one day per fortnight that the court has deemed they should have access. Always assuming, of course, that a) it's all right with his new girlfriend and *her* children, b) it's all right with his ex-wife, her new boyfriend and *his* children and c) they're back by 6 because, after all, it *is* a school day tomorrow.

ROLE MODELS

In April 2009, the new President of the USA and his wife arrived in the UK for the G20 summit. Michelle Obama took the opportunity to go to a girls' school in North London and addressed the pupils there. She urged them to have the 'confidence and fortitude' to determine their own success, saying: 'You, too, can control your own destiny.' She then singled out three prominent women as suitable role models for the girls: the Queen, Gordon Brown's wife and Alistair Darling's wife. So, that's one woman who was born into a position of prominence in society, and two women who, however admirable their many personal qualities, would appear to have achieved their prominence by, er, being married to prominent men. Interesting choices.

PARENTS AND CHILDREN

Of course, in today's Britain, these are often one and the same. The face of the family is changing and, sometimes, the face turns out to be that of a 13-year-old, as in the case of Alfie. He was the barely teenage boy from Eastbourne who hit the headlines in 2009, when he thought, along with everyone else, that he'd got his 15-year-old girlfriend Chantelle pregnant. If Alfie *had* been the father, he'd have made Chantelle pregnant at the tender age of 12. After paternity tests, though, it emerged that Alfie wasn't the father – a 15-year-old boy called Tyler, on the same estate, was. So that's all right, then.

For many, the most shocking aspect of this story was the fact it didn't take place in Middlesbrough.

New father Tyler revealed he lost his virginity to Chantelle during a one-night stand, after spending the evening drinking at her home. The 15-year-old said: 'I didn't use any contraception, but Chantelle told me she would take the morning-after pill. But I only slept with her the once. All my mates have been teasing me, but it's not funny.'

No. It's not. Sometimes it seems that the Taliban aren't *always* wrong.

WHERE TO GET FAMILY PLANNING ADVICE

Should you find yourself in the position of being a 13-year-old who thinks he's got his 15-year-old girlfriend pregnant, Social Services stand ready to offer advice on what to do. They will have a pre-printed leaflet readily available which

- explains the correct procedure for contacting Max Clifford
- provides a handy pull-out-and-keep list of the direct-line numbers of all the editors of major tabloid newspapers
- includes a table of comparative rates for exclusives, semi-exclusives, life-story serialisation rights for family members, template family photo syndication agreements, etc.

Statistics tell us that almost one-quarter of the population (some 15 million individuals) are under the age of 19. Between the hours of 3.15 p.m. and 5.00 p.m., Monday to Friday, many of them are on the move and can be spotted on public transport. People of a nervous disposition, and those who, for some reason, dislike open-mouthed gum-chewing, loud iPods, spots and robust Anglo-Saxon language are well advised to plan their own journeys outside these hours. There are, after all, only so many times one can expose oneself to conversations that go, 'So I was like – wha'? An' he was like – wha' you mean, wha'? An' I was like – wha'ever. An' he was like – slag', without going completely bonkers.

FAMILY LIFE

Because of changing attitudes to divorce and separation, family patterns have altered markedly over the last 20 years. Some sociologists believe that, as long as post-split relationships can be kept civilised, far from signalling the end of the family unit, they may have actually *revived* the concept of the extended family. Take the case of Karen Matthews in Dewsbury. Because of her multiple relationships, her children could derive great comfort and security from their many uncles – especially her 9-year-old daughter, Shannon, who must have felt very comfortable and secure hidden in the drawers of her uncle's divan.

Nowadays, the average teenager's extended family could be taken to include their father and/or stepfather, their mother and/ or stepmother, their step- and/or half-brothers and sisters, their half-sister's father, their half-sister's father's former girlfriend and her children, their half-brother's mother, their half-brother's mother's former boyfriend and his children, and their grandfather or step-grandfather, and grandmother or step-grandmother, on both sides, and his or her new partner(s).

FAMILY RELATIONSHIPS

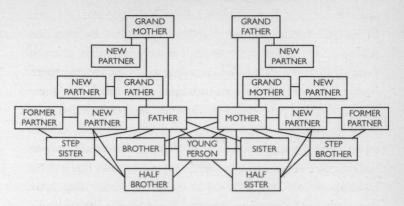

Family relationships today: If you half-close your eyes,
the diagram looks a bit like the Forth Bridge

The Forth Bridge: Really quite stable

With such a web of familial, half-familial and step-familial interconnection, some sociologists argue that, in the long run, society may actually become more stable. Whether or not that's true, at least the chances of getting enough people together at Christmas to finally play a game of 'Diplomacy' are now massively increased.

CHILDREN AT PLAY

In the UK, children tend not to play outside, like they used to in days gone by. This is partly due to laziness, computers, allergies and a widespread lack of insultingly simple toys made entirely from wood. But it's mainly due to tabloid newspapers, which have succeeded in creating mass hysteria about paedophiles lurking on every street corner. While it is true that they may well be some of the vilest, sickest elements of our society, tabloid newspapers remain a fact of modern life. There's no evidence that children are any less safe now than they ever were, but lack of evidence has never stopped the tabloids from recklessly feeding their readers' fears, if they think it might boost circulation.

As a result, many parents tend to over-compensate for their children's lack of freedom in terms of outside activities, by buying more, and better, home entertainment systems such as TVs, DVD players and laptops. However, such exclusively sedentary pastimes have serious health implications, thereby allowing the tabloid newspapers yet another opportunity to run a recurring scare story – namely, how unfit today's children are, and how this means they'll probably be the first generation to die before their parents. Unfortunately, there's quite a lot of evidence that suggests this is a distinct possibility – so, just for once, it's a case of 'Tabloid Headline In Having-A-Point Shock!'

EDUCATION

The law used to state that children between the ages of 5 and 16 must attend school. This will soon be raised to 18, in order to better achieve… something or other. Whether it does indeed achieve something or other remains to be seen. Entirely coincidentally, this change may also help to keep the unemployment figures looking marginally better at a time when, thanks to the credit squeeze and the worldwide financial outlook, they're beginning to rise alarmingly again (except in the field of unemployment-figure-counting, which is, apparently, booming).

Many different types of school exist in the UK. There are the so-called Public Schools, which, unlike those in the USA are not, in fact, 'public schools' but are, effectively, Private Schools (see below). Next come the Private Schools, which include the Public Schools (see above) and are, funnily enough, open to the public (if they can afford the fees). Then there are the non-fee-paying State Schools, so-called because some of the schools are, sadly, in a bit of a state.

PUBLIC SCHOOLS

The most famous English Public Schools are Eton and Harrow. Pupils at these schools can usually be distinguished by the traditional (and unashamedly old-fashioned) clothes they wear, which make them relatively easy to spot in the average crowd.

NB The pupils from Eton are the two on the left

These rather formal dress habits, established early on, are often carried through by former pupils into later life.

But not always.

Perhaps the most famous Old Etonians in the country today are David Cameron, Boris Johnson (above) and Princes William and Harry. Eighteen former prime ministers are also past pupils of the school. Old Etonians are often referred to as 'Eamonns', as in 'Eamonn Old Etonian, don't you know.'

Famous Old Harrovians include the late Humphrey Lyttleton, who for many years was the King of Jordan, and King Hussein, who for many years was the host of Radio 4's evergreen panel show *I'm Sorry I Haven't a Clue*. Though, thinking about it, it was possibly the other way round. Anyway, to date, the school has produced only seven British prime ministers. They want to pull their finger out, don't they? The former PM John Major went to Harrow in the 1960s. But just the once, and even then it was only because he dozed off on the Metropolitan line and missed his stop.

Scotland has a number of famous 'Public Schools', famed for their spartan conditions and 'tough-love' approach to education. They pride themselves on their ability to prepare otherwise rather weedy and ineffectual children for the harsh, bruising, competitive, cut-throat world of, say, Royalty. The Prince of Wales attended Gordonstoun, a school set in the remote wastes of Morayshire –

as opposed to the conveniently located wastes of that ilk. He was the first member of the Royal Family to attend a regular school (if one can call it that), previous generations having muddled along somehow with governesses and private tutors. Gordonstoun was chosen for the Prince by his father, the Duke of Edinburgh, on the basis that he himself had been there and it never did him any harm, although this is obviously only a matter of opinion.

Charles has been fairly open about the fact that he didn't enjoy his life at Gordonstoun and found the daily routine there tough. Since leaving, however, he hasn't done too badly in terms of enjoying his life and *not* finding his daily routine tough, so swings and roundabouts, eh, Sir? When looking for the sort of school his hero James Bond would have attended, Ian Fleming settled on Gordonstoun. Although, since Bond is a fictional character, it's hard to draw any particular conclusions from that. Hardly worth mentioning, really. Funny how it always seems to crop up in books like this, though, isn't it?

A CURIOUS 'PUBLIC SCHOOL' FACT

Sir Eric Anderson retired as Headmaster of Eton in 2009. During his long career he worked at Gordonstoun, where he taught the young Prince Charles. He taught at Fettes College in Edinburgh, where he was Housemaster to the young Tony Blair. He then went on to be Headmaster at Eton during the period when one of his charges was David Cameron. Which meant that for a brief period when Blair and Cameron were leaders of their parties, Sir Eric had been a guiding influence on the lives of the then Prime Minister, the Leader of Her Majesty's Opposition and the heir to the throne. He must be rubbish.

STATE SCHOOLS AND ACADEMIES

Most State Schools have their funding provided entirely by the State. Except those that don't. New Labour introduced the idea of Academies, which are publicly funded, but receive some private sponsorship from wealthy individuals or companies who want to put their name to something perceived as being worthwhile, so fair enough. The scheme was designed to provide a shot in the arm for otherwise failing schools, and was intended to replace the system of 'City Technology Colleges', or CTCs, introduced by the Conservatives. Under this scheme, some schools were rebranded and given names sure to swell the breast of any pupil with pride, such as 'Dixons CTC'. Its pupils may not have known anything about a given subject but, when asked a question, they were only too happy to go and fetch the manager. Three cheers for the old Dixonians!

When the revised New Labour scheme was launched in 2000, the schools were known as 'City Academies', but they are now known simply as 'Academies'.*

The most remarkable feature of this schools initiative is that it has the distinction of being just about the only cheesy New Labour bandwagon that Sir Richard Branson appears never to have jumped on. So the 'Sir Richard Branson School of Entrepreneurship and Photo-Opportunitivism' (where optional specialist courses will include 'Beginners' Beards', 'Advanced Knitwear' and 'Picking Up The Person You're Supposed To Be Just Posing With') is yet to be founded.

---

* As a general rule, the only reason for the Government to relaunch and rebrand an initiative is because it hasn't actually been working. In 2006, more than half of the Government's 'flagship' Academies in London found themselves featuring on the league table of the worst schools in the country. So, the question of whether rebranding is a good thing or not is, quite literally, academic.

Branson: For some reason, when presented with
a photo-opportunity, he finds it hard to resist trying
to pick up the person with whom he's posing…

… although sometimes even he has to admit defeat

COMPREHENSIVE
AND GRAMMAR SCHOOLS

The majority of schools in the state education system (around ninety per cent) are classified as 'Comprehensive' schools. This means that they do not select children on the basis of academic achievement or aptitude. However, in a few areas there are still 'islands' of selectivity, where Grammar Schools, which are allowed to select their intake of pupils by ability using the '11-plus' exam, continue to exist. Those in favour say that competition against a peer group isn't a bad thing. Critics argue that the experience of being told you've effectively 'failed' an examination at this crucial formative stage can be damaging to a young person. They claim that the system risks instilling a chippy or resentful attitude towards the world in general that can take many years to shake off. But evidence for this side of the argument is not readily available – as it happens, former Deputy Prime Minister John Prescott failed *his* 11-plus yet, in his case, it clearly didn't have any lasting... Oh, hang on.

In the old days, public schools were the natural breeding ground for the politicians of the future. Mrs Thatcher's time in office, however, was notable for the number of former state-school pupils she had in her Cabinet. This was, naturally, seen by the private-school contingent as an affront, and for them represented a worrying flirtation with meritocracy by the party. Deciding to bide their time, in due course they were able to re-establish their stranglehold to such an extent that, among the members of the current Shadow Cabinet at the time of going to print, the following could be found:

- David Cameron (Leader of the Opposition) – Eton
- George Osborne (Shadow Chancellor) – St Paul's
- Nick Herbert (Environment and Food and Rural Affairs) – Haileybury

- Alan Duncan (Shadow Leader of the House) –
  Merchant Taylors'
- Jeremy Hunt (Culture, Media and Sport) – Charterhouse
- Cheryl Gillan (Wales) – Cheltenham Ladies College
- Francis Maude (Cabinet Office) – Abingdon School
- Andrew Mitchell (International Development) – Rugby
- David Willetts (Innovation, Universities and Skills) –
  King Edward's School
- Owen Patterson (Northern Ireland) – Radley College
- Lord Strathclyde (Leader of the Lords) –
  Wellington College
- Wayne Scroggs (Intelligence Gathering) –
  Barnsley Polytechnic

(OK, that last one was made up, but you get the idea.)

PARENTAL CHOICE

The Government has placed great emphasis on parents choosing which school their child attends. Unfortunately, the choice parents in some areas have been faced with recently is limited to choosing which ballot their child's name goes into. Which many parents feel is not quite the same thing, somehow. Some local authorities were quick to spot the potential up-side of such ballots for school places: from their point of view, it completely does away with the need to sit through all those boring appeals for places at the most popular schools. A quick 'I'm very sorry, it's random, you see, so there's nothing we can do' and that's it – phone down, job done. Another National Lottery in the making. (Note to TV producers: that wasn't a suggestion.)

NATIONAL EXAMINATIONS

Politically speaking, education has always been a 'hot topic'. New Labour famously came to power in 1997 promising that its

EXAMS – A SIMPLE GUIDE

In the UK, the national examination system has been described by the Government as 'relatively straightforward': at age 16 pupils take the General Certificate of Secondary Education (GCSE – still often referred to as O levels) – except in Scotland, where they take the Scottish Qualification Authority (SQA) Standard Grade Examinations. At age 17 and 18, students go on to take General Certificates of Education at Advanced Level (AGCEs – still often referred to as A levels) – except in Scotland, where they sit Higher or Advanced Higher Grades (HG or AHG) – and/or students take Advanced Subsidiary (AS) levels gained by completing three AS 'units', three AS units being considered the equivalent of one-half of an AGCE. See? What could be simpler than that? (Answer: the mind of the person who thought up the system, obviously.)

three priorities would be 'Education, education, education'. The obsession with targets and the attempt to measure what is, in essence, unmeasurable meant it was soon clear that 'Examination, examination, examination' would have been much more appropriate as a headline-grabbing sound bite. In New Labour's ideal world, pupils would start school at 5 years old, and be tested immediately, whether they can read and write or not, just to get them into the spirit of the thing, really. This would then be followed up by national testing at age 6, exam-based assessments at 7, testing at age 8, examinations at 9, testing and assessments at 10, age 11 exams, testing at 12 followed by assessments at 13, national testing at age 14, mock exams at 15, and national examinations at 16, 17 and 18. In the event, the Government had to content itself, in England at least, with tests at age 7, 11 and 14 – with national exams at 16, 17 and 18, of course (see opposite for details – if you haven't lost the will to live yet).

Inevitably, national testing at age 14 was abolished, as from 2009 – just as everyone had said it would have to be. One side effect of the abolition is that secondary-school teachers may now find themselves in serious danger of being allowed to actually teach their subject in their own way, and in an interesting manner. Many critics of the current system are fond of quoting the old saying 'You don't fatten a pig by weighing it, but you have to kill it to make sausages.' Yes indeed. Whatever that means.

In recent years, there have been occasions when the examination system has almost descended into farce, with one American company, ETS Europe, having its contract terminated in 2008 after failing to deliver exam results in time. Steps have now been taken to make sure this never happens again: every child sitting an examination from now on will be *guaranteed* to receive their results before their 30th birthday.

HIGHER EDUCATION

Higher education at a college or university is currently taken up by around thirty per cent of students – the remaining seventy per cent having dropped out after failing to understand the examination system outlined above.

Once upon a time, the cost of a university education was borne by the state. The Conservatives under Margaret Thatcher (MA Oxon.) and then John Major (6 O levels, Rutlish Comprehensive, and then correspondence course) shied away from introducing fees for students. Tony 'Education, education, education' Blair had no such scruples and went ahead with their introduction, drawing up the relevant legislation in 2004, with the provisions taking effect from the academic year 2006–2007. Some people were surprised by this, as his party had declared their opposition

BAD SCIENCE

In recent years, academic attention in the UK has specifically focused on the teaching of science. Schools have been encouraged to specialise in teaching this subject, extra funds being provided to make up for the UK's perceived shortfall in this important area. There are a number of theories as to why this might be, but so far no one appears to have addressed the central cause. The real reason why young people today know less about science than previous generations did is 'Dave'.

In the old days, if you came in late and were looking for something to watch before going to bed, you would tune in to find that, invariably, the only programmes shown on telly after 11.30 at night were the ones from the Open University. These generally featured a bearded man in a cheesecloth shirt with an oversized collar who, after welcoming you to 'Intermediate Chemistry: Unit 205', went on to explain, at some length, either covalent bonding or fractional distillation, in a mesmerisingly unhurried manner. It was therefore possible, over several years and hundreds of nocturnal bowls of cornflakes, to absorb a substantial amount of basic, black-and-white science by the process of osmosis (which was, incidentally, covered in Unit 204). But ever since the arrival of the TV channel formerly known as UKTVG2 (you can see why they changed the name), *Jack Dee Live at the Apollo* has been on late-night TV more or less every night of the year.

Public misunderstanding of science

So if Professor Marcus de Sautoy, the current holder of Oxford University's Simonyi Professorship for the Public Understanding of Science happens to be reading this: there's your answer right there, mate. Get rid of Dave.

to the fees many times during the preceding few years. Indeed, the Labour manifesto of just three years earlier, for the 2001 election, had stated categorically: 'We have no plans to introduce university top-up fees, and have legislated to prevent their introduction.' The Government denied that it had gone back on its word (as if!) and insisted that the manifesto had been meant to refer to the parliament of 2001–2005 and that, since the measures didn't come into effect until 2006, it could not be said to be a broken promise.

This shameless weaselling convinced only the same terminally naive individuals who had been persuaded by the 'I did not have sexual relations with that woman' line used by Bill Clinton a few years earlier. Supporters of Tony Blair were quick to point out that, on coming to power, he hadn't said his priorities would be 'Free education, free education, free education', had he? No, exactly. So there.

THE GAP YEAR

It has become increasingly common for students to take a year off, known as a 'Gap Year', before or after going to college or 'uni', as university is now irritatingly called by people under the age of 35 (or 'the Varsity' by people over the age of 75). Research has shown that these are the same people who, when ordering something in a café, have a tendency to begin their sentences with 'Can I get...' instead of 'Can I have...' As in:

Customer: Can I get a latte, please?
Café owner: Well, not really, no – you see, on the whole,
             we find it works better if you stay on that
             side of the counter, and I get it for you.

The Gap Year is a year spent travelling, seeing the world and 'finding yourself', which will traditionally involve at least four of the following elements:

- Long, much-delayed and uncomfortable flights on some of the world's least safety-conscious airlines

- Getting comprehensively ripped off by a dodgy-looking taxi driver from Laos, whether in Laos or not

- Eventually having to be downright rude in order to get shot of the two creepily insistent German dental students who keep suggesting you all travel together – 'So we can hang out and share a room and everything, ja?'

- At least one, like, truly amazing head-massage, yeah, on a beach on a remote island with a name that sounds like a rude word in English

- A month spent 'crashing' on an ex's cousin's floor in Sydney whilst trying to recover from a violent bout of the same amoebic dysentery which kicked in on day five, and which will return at random intervals at least twice a year, for the next ten years or so.

YOUNG PEOPLE AND WORK

Young people often have part-time jobs while still at school, the most common being newspaper delivery, otherwise known as a 'paper round'. Some parents believe that allowing a child to get up at 5.30 every morning and lug an extraordinarily heavy bag full of newspapers around the neighbourhood in the pouring rain before heading off to school and trying desperately not to fall asleep all day is, somehow, character-forming. The Victorians probably regarded going up chimneys as character-forming, too.

At the age of 16, young people can choose to take weekend jobs in shops to earn their money. Many are put to work on the tills, where the tradition has developed of the young person seizing the opportunity to organise a rota of groups of friends who turn up on several occasions over the course of a day, just to keep them company.

The topics of the ensuing discussions range widely: from which boy (or girl) each member of the group happens to fancy at the moment, and why, all the way through to which boy (or girl) happens to fancy each member of the group at the moment, and why. It is clear that the participants in this ritual consider it the height of rudeness for a mere 'customer' to interrupt them, and members of the public should be aware that no amount of elaborate tutting or ostentatious watch-checking is likely to elicit any response at all.

HEALTH HAZARDS FOR YOUNG PEOPLE

In recent years, the use of drugs and other addictive substances has been on the increase among young people. Basically, the clue's in the title – 'addictive'.

TOBACCO PRODUCTS

A number of Government initiatives have tried to get to grips with the problems of tobacco use with varying degrees of success, although banning the advertising of cigarettes may have had some effect.

Tobacco manufacturers were prevented from advertising their products directly many years ago, but quickly diverted their advertising budgets into the sponsorship of major sporting events, rooting their brand names in the public consciousness by plastering their logos on anything that moved, and many things that didn't. One of the early decisions of the Blair Government when it came to power in 1997 was to ban such sponsorship by tobacco companies on the not-unreasonable grounds that they were simply using it to get round the advertising ban. It subsequently turned out that, after some intensive lobbying, Tony Blair had agreed to a single exemption from this new rule: Formula One motor racing. The precise reason for this exemption being granted has never been fully established. However, it soon emerged that Bernie Ecclestone, the massively wealthy but tiny man in charge of Formula One, had made a donation of one million pounds to Labour Party funds around that time. When this fact came to light, it prompted Tony Blair to go on television and famously declare to John Humphrys: 'Look, people think I'm a pretty straight sort of guy, and I am.'

Blair: A pretty straight sort of guy?

Prior to this whole incident, in terms of public perception, that might just have been the case, but it was certainly not so afterwards. In the end, public opinion obliged the Labour Party to return Bernie Ecclestone's money (although Formula One continued to enjoy the controversial sponsorship exemption), and Tony Blair never tried the 'pretty straight sort of guy' line again. It wasn't until the whole 'We have evidence that Iraq is developing weapons of mass destruction' business that people began to realise fully just what a 'pretty straight sort of guy' he really was.

Amongst the adult population, the number of smokers is falling, but more young people of school age are smoking. Interestingly, thanks to Government transport initiatives, it seems more young people nowadays are also cycling to school. No research into the link has yet been undertaken, but it is becoming increasingly clear that having to visit the bike sheds at least twice a day may be proving too much of a temptation for many of today's impressionable or weak-willed youngsters.

In 2007, it was made illegal to sell tobacco products to anyone under the age of 18. In 2009, incidents were reported in the press involving parents who were turned away at the tobacco counter in supermarkets because they wanted to buy cigarettes for themselves but happened to have their children with them at the time. Thus has British society apparently delegated to supermarket checkout persons the role of deciding who is and who is not likely to be the sort of person who would attempt to buy fags on behalf of their child. Unquestionably, supermarket checkout persons are the best people to perform this kind of character assessment, as anyone who has ever shopped in a supermarket can confirm.*

On the subject of the possibly excessive nanny-state-ish tendencies of supermarket staff, in May 2009 the Daily Telegraph *reported the case of a shopper in the Halifax branch of Asda who was asked by an assistant for proof of age when they tried to buy some teaspoons. The shopper was astonished, and wondered aloud what possible reason there could be for such a policy. Whereupon the shop assistant responded that it was because someone had once been murdered with a spoon. Indeed they have: back in July 2004, St Albans Crown Court heard the case of a man accused of having killed someone with a spoon – admittedly a dessert spoon, but hey. However, spoon-related crime of this sort is very rare. So please – don't have nightmares.*

Smoking is now prohibited in public buildings and workplaces throughout the UK, which is why on any winter's day it's possible to spot sad little clumps of smokers gathered together on the pavements outside offices. The appearance of these tragic-looking groups is like nothing so much as those penguins in the documentaries that are endlessly repeated on the wildlife channels. Here, we witness all the wonder of the collective wisdom of the colony, an instinct that wordlessly ensures that the individuals on the outside of the group who have borne the brunt of the chilling effect of the winds are, after a while, allowed to shuffle themselves gradually closer to the centre to keep warm. In this way, as the weeks go by, the precious body-heat is conserved as they huddle together to await the first longed-for signs of the coming of spring. (Copyright D. Attenborough, 1995)

ALCOHOL

The phenomenon known as 'binge drinking' (a phrase much-beloved of tabloid journalists) has become an important social issue in recent years. A precise definition of what is meant by the term in various different societies has proved elusive, but the International Centre for Alcohol Policies has published the following table, based on surveys conducted amongst drinkers in each country:

AMERICANS SAY	Four drinks per occasion for women, five or more drinks per occasion for men, on at least one day in the last thirty
CANADIANS SAY	Eight drinks within the same day
SWEDES SAY	Half a bottle of spirits or two bottles of wine on the same occasion

FINNS SAY	Six or more bottles of beer per session
BRITISH SAY	Whatimeizzit leshava nuther saymergain pleashe mate

New relaxed licensing laws, introduced in 2003, were designed to bring the UK more into line with continental drinking habits. Prior to their introduction, the Government was at pains to emphasise the belief that the new laws would, in due course, lead to a 'café culture'. Extending opening hours would, they claimed, avoid the situation where people drink to excess in the hour between 10 p.m. and 11 p.m. in order to squeeze in as many drinks as possible before the pubs close. In this, the measures succeeded to a degree: recent figures show that drinking to excess now takes place in the hour between 11 p.m. and 12 a.m. in order to squeeze in as many drinks as possible before the pubs close.*

There is, of course, a difference between a 'binge drinker' and being an alcoholic, although when faced with a loud, aggressive, swearing drunk and his vomiting girlfriend outside a pub at midnight, it's not necessarily one that is likely to be appreciated.

---

* *During an episode of* Have I Got News for You, *Boris Johnson speculated that 'Binge' would be quite a good name for an alcoholic drink. When it was pointed out by Paul Merton that headlines such as 'Binge Drinking Kills' would be unlikely to help with the marketing of the product, Boris immediately and graciously conceded that this was, perhaps, not one of his better ideas. Rather, it was one of his more crackpot suggestions. Still, he's Mayor of London – what's the worst that could happen?*

However, the BBC website has the following suggestion for anyone having trouble trying to work out if they are an alcoholic or merely a 'binge drinker':

> 'Put yourself in a situation where you would normally want a drink – and see what happens when you deny yourself.'

ALCOHOL AND THE NHS

Bad news:	Good News:
every year the NHS spends nearly TWO BILLION POUNDS treating alcohol-related illnesses	every year the Government raises SEVEN BILLION POUNDS through taxes on alcohol

Is that an unduly cynical comparison to include? Probably. Cheers, anyway.

DRUGS

Drugs such as heroin, cocaine, ecstasy, amphetamines and cannabis, despite being illegal, are widely available in the UK. There are frequent calls for such drugs to be made legal, thereby removing at a stroke the ability of criminals to profit from the trade. Despite the obvious and somewhat cynical appeal of the levels of tax revenue that legalised drugs could bring in (see 'Alcohol and the NHS' above), there are no plans for this to happen. So far as we know. But the Government's going to have to raise revenue from just about everywhere if it's ever to stand a chance of paying for the bail-out of the banks, so watch this space.

YOUNG PEOPLE AND POLITICS

The age at which people can vote in elections is 18, but there is an apparent reluctance among the young to exercise their franchise. Figures show that, in recent years, only twenty per cent of first-time voters actually used their vote in any given election. Politicians of all parties are increasingly aware that young people are becoming detached from, and indifferent to, the political process – wow, who knew? Hence some politicians' repeated and increasingly desperate attempts to jazz up their image, by doing things like not wearing a tie, being on Facebook, signing up for Twitter, and shagging one of the Cheeky Girls.

Whilst young people are clearly disenchanted with party politics, this does not mean that they are unaware of the larger issues affecting society today. For instance, many young people are increasingly militant about environmental matters. Often they will express more awareness than their parents of the issues surrounding CO_2 emissions, and it's not uncommon for teenagers to try to persuade the rest of the family of the benefits of a greener lifestyle. They will actively challenge what they regard as the family's continuing overreliance on their car, right up until the moment when they ring to ask if they can be picked up from Izzy's in about half an hour, 'cos it was games today and I twisted my ankle a bit and I'm really tired and anyway I've got my bag and everything, oh, *please*…

Every so often an event comes along that seems to cause young people to mobilise in a concerted fashion. One such occasion was the staging of the G20 Summit in London in April 2009, and the associated demonstrations by 'Anti Staging Of London Economic Summit' protestors (the acronym tends not to get used). The role the banks played in the recent financial chaos and their subsequent behaviour brought people out onto the streets in large numbers to get the message of their complete rejection of hard-line capitalist values across.

G20 summit protests: Not the language
***Daily Telegraph* readers would have chosen,**
but a sentiment common to both groups

If an indication were needed of the level of popular support for the protests, it was revealed that Russell Brand himself was there on the day, mingling anonymously with the ordinary people. He was wearing dark glasses, a woolly hat pulled down low and a scarf covering his face.

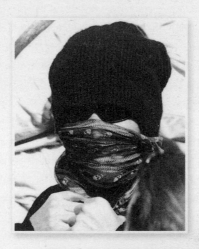

Brand: Anonymous

Quite quickly, however, he ditched the shades and the scarf. But was it because

> a) he had been recognised, or
> b) he hadn't been recognised?

Brand: You decide

One might have thought Brand would have been too busy with his usual hobbies (no real need to chronicle what they are – I think we all know by now) to bother going on a demo, but apparently not. How astonished his publicists must have been when they realised they'd been completely outmanoeuvred by the Metropolitan Police, whose tactics (which included covering the numbers on their uniforms with black tape so they couldn't be identified, kettling, slapping the faces and batoning the legs of women protestors, and pushing over randomly selected individuals one of whom subsequently died) virtually guaranteed that they would hog the front pages for the next week or so.

Surveys show that young people are more likely than ever to have been involved in some sort of fundraising for a good cause or collecting money for charity – indeed a recent one revealed that fifty per cent had taken part in such activities.

The level of involvement and commitment varies, however. For example, many schools now hold 'non-uniform' days on various occasions throughout the year, when children are 'invited' to wear their own clothes to school, and of course, which child would wish to be left out, and which parent would want them to be? In return for this 'privilege', the school 'suggests' a donation to a good cause of the school's choosing.

Some parents feel rather resentful at being manoeuvred into stumping up in this way, and are tempted to view it as tantamount to an obligatory 'charity tax', with the money going to a charity of someone else's choosing. It's not clear if that's the sort of thing that's meant by 'involvement in fundraising for a good cause', but if it ticks a box, then who could possibly be churlish enough to object on the grounds of, say, feeling uncomfortable at an apparent attempt at moral coercion?

In an effort to increase awareness of social issues amongst young people, the Government has made 'Citizenship' part of the National

Curriculum. Normally, of course, putting something like that on the curriculum is the kiss of death for the subject as far as the pupils are concerned, and there is some debate about whether 'Citizenship' can in fact be taught like any other subject. Ministers appear to think so, but critics of the plan say that it can't, and that the only real way for a young person to absorb the principles of citizenship is by example. If they're right then perhaps that explains a lot, given the examples of 'citizenship' that are displayed nightly on TV in the soaps, and which tend to have a lasting impact on attitudes among the younger generation. Know what I mean, you slag?

MEDIA IN THE UK

NEWSPAPERS

The first-ever newspapers in the UK appeared in the eighteenth century, and the most famous of these still in existence is *The Times*. It was first published under the title *The Daily Universal Register*, and the newspaper today bears very little resemblance to the original edition, because, of course, *The Times*, it is, er, they are a-changing.

Daily newspapers quickly turned into little more than a series of paid-for advertisements with the occasional news story attached, and it is this reliance on advertising revenue that has seen the steady collapse of the newspaper industry, as readers and advertisers migrate to the internet. Nevertheless, the Press still exerts great influence on the major issues of the day, such as the eviction of *Big Brother* housemates and the sacking of BBC presenters.

It is always worth remembering the traditional editorial stance of a newspaper, or the sort of reader it is pandering to, before judging the accuracy of its reporting. So here is a quick guide to the editorial stance of some of the UK's biggest selling titles. And *The Independent*.

THE SUN	The newsprint equivalent of an arse on a photocopier: hideous but still quite funny
THE MIRROR	Can't quite remove the stain of Piers Morgan
DAILY EXPRESS	Asylum seekers are to blame
THE INDEPENDENT	Capitalism is to blame
DAILY MAIL	Will you die of cancer before house prices recover?
THE TIMES	The Sun with better grammar
THE GUARDIAN	Essential reading for local council diversity outreach officers
DAILY TELEGRAPH	Traditionally focused on outstanding A-level results of blonde totty; now famous throughout the world since MPs' Expenses scandal for searing investigative journalism (or highest bidders for stolen Commons data)
THE STAR	Text messages 'n' slags

TELEVISION

The UK has dozens of different TV channels. Or, rather, the UK has dozens of not-really-very-different TV channels. To be brutally honest, many more than is actually necessary. In the early 1980s, somebody in a position of power decided that there wasn't quite enough drivel being broadcast to the public, and that certain minority groups needed their own drivel, specifically designed to infuriate and patronise them. As a result, some new television channels were created to provide drivel in the early morning. Despite the uniformly appalling quality of every single second of Breakfast Television, the Powers That Be decided that what the nation needed was even more hours of similar drivel. Within a few years, 24-hour, multi-channel drivel was being pumped into millions of British homes, simultaneously enriching a number of media moguls and culturally impoverishing the entire population. Tragic though it may seem, British television is still the best in the world.

A newcomer to Britain's TV schedules would be grateful for a helpful guide to the kind of programming each channel provides, but they will have to make do with this one:

BBC ONE	Soaps, chat shows, big sporting events, mainstream entertainment shows which boost the businesses of famous people like Sir Alan Sugar and Lord Andrew Lord Lloyd Webber Lord. But it's totally different from ITV1.
BBC TWO	Poetry, classical music, gardening, snooker, Jeremy Paxman in a mood.
ITV1	Soaps, chat shows, big sporting events, mainstream entertainment shows which boost the businesses of famous people like Simon Cowell and Marco Pierre White. But it's totally different from BBC One.
CHANNEL 4	Property, cookery, property, cookery, cookery, property, people showing doctors their genitals and Jimmy Carr.
FIVE	CSI, NCIS, CIS, RSI, OCD, SRN, MRSA, Was Hitler Gay?

ITV2	Trashy teen-mum/celebrity dirtbag-based rubbish. But it's completely different from BBC Three.
BBC THREE	No, it isn't.
BBC FOUR	Trains, boy scouts, popular beat-combos, thermos flasks, tartan blankets.
ITV3	Er… Morse, Hart to Hart… dunno. Quincy?
ITV4	No one knows.
SKY ONE	Ross Kemp trembling in a trench, pretending to be hard.
SKY SPORTS	On paper, mouth-watering top-of-the-table Premiership clashes. In reality, Blackburn v. Stoke.
MORE 4	Daily Show with Jon Stewart (three minutes of jokes and a bald guy plugging a book).
DAVE	Testosterone-fuelled, male-dominated panel shows where women aren't allowed to compete, etc., etc.
DAVE-JA VU	Quite possibly the worst name ever conceived for anything, ever.
QVC	Hang on, this actually looks quite interesting. There's some sort of Pinteresque drama on at the moment, about an awful couple locked in an apparently loveless relationship… The dialogue is authentically banal, and the whole technique is satisfyingly gritty and unglamorous… Oh, my mistake, they're selling saucepans.

PART THREE

THE UK TODAY: A PROFILE

POPULATION OF THE UK

It's really quite big. Big enough to mean that there are fewer places in good schools than there are pupils who want one, fewer seats on trains than passengers who want one and, in some areas, fewer beds in Intensive Care Units than patients who want one. The UK population estimate for July 2009 is 61,113,205 (less the eight who've just died during the first half of this sentence, because they couldn't get a bed in Intensive Care). You may think that 61,113,205 – sorry, 61,113,197 – is a suspiciously precise figure, but it is a figure provided by the CIA, and those guys know this sort of stuff.*

Among the other fascinating facts the CIA can tell you about the UK is that the country is slightly smaller than the state of Oregon, which is home to just 3.7 million people. But bear in mind that the population of Oregon is almost entirely made up of Americans, so obviously they each need a fair bit more room to manoeuvre.

---

* They also know lots of other stuff too, some of it relating to extraordinary rendition – but it won't be made public in your lifetime and, on the whole, it's probably best not to ask too many questions about it, or you'll end up on a list of people who are never granted visas, so you won't be allowed to enter the USA as long as you live.

The UK population is projected to keep on growing: the Office of National Statistics recently calculated that, by 2081, the population of the UK could rise to 108.7 million. And you think it's hard to find a parking space *now*…

Some eighty-four per cent of the population of the UK lives in England, while the Scots make up eight per cent, the Welsh five per cent, and Northern Irelanders three per cent. (Be honest – you actually added them up in your head to make sure they came to one hundred per cent, didn't you? Well, they do, so there.) Although the overall population has been increasing, over the last twenty years some areas have experienced a decline, such as the North East of England. Sunderland's in the North East, isn't it?

These estimated population figures are complicated by the fact that the birth rate and the death rate are both falling. In other words, people have stopped being born, and people have also stopped dying. No, hang on… Sorry. Bit of a heavy lunch. In other words, fewer babies are being born (despite the best efforts of Britain's teenagers), and fewer old people are dying (although here the numbers may have been affected by the arrest and subsequent demise of Harold Shipman). As a result of these trends, there are currently more people aged over 60 than there are under 16, although you wouldn't know it from the sort of stuff Channel 4 keeps churning out.

LIFE EXPECTANCY

The current world average life expectancy is about 66 years. This makes the UK figure of 76 for men and 81 for women look not too bad, and means the country is ranked 37th in the world for life expectancy (out of a possible 221). Interestingly, or maybe not, four of the top five countries on the list are Macau, Andorra, Singapore and San Marino. So the conclusion is clear – move to a small, boring country and you'll end up living longer. And it's more or less guaranteed to end up seeming a lot longer, too.

Scientists estimate that human life expectancy was at its lowest during the Bronze Age, from 3,300 to 1,200 BC, when it was about 18. Which means that there will have been countless unlucky people who snuffed it well before they had the chance to experience their first pint, tattoo or provisional driving licence.

This Bronze Age life expectancy was significantly lower than in the Upper Palaeolithic era (about 40,000 to 10,000 years earlier), when it's reckoned to have been around 33. No doubt the Leader of the Opposition at the time (ever the cynical opportunist) would have taken full advantage of the Government's discomfiture when the information came to light:

> According to the latest figures, people in previous eras could expect to live twice as long as people today. [Some Hon. Members: Oh, oh!] When is the party opposite going to stop blaming everything on previous administrations? Why won't they come clean and admit it: as far as prehistoric life expectancy is concerned, they have completely failed to do away with boom and bust?
>
> [Hansard]

So, packed as it was with smelly, inarticulate 18-year-olds (no change there, then), Bronze Age Britain was even more teen-centric a place than the bench outside Threshers. From then on, life expectancy rose steadily. For children, it went up dramatically during the Industrial Revolution, in the late eighteenth and early nineteenth centuries. In London, the percentage of children who died before the age of 5 dropped from an astonishing rate of seventy-five per cent in 1740 to thirty-two per cent in 1820. This was undoubtedly a good thing because it meant that, later in the century, there were many more children available when the Victorians needed something to clean out the chimney, unblock the sharp end of the loom and get right into the fiddly bits of the coalmine.

THE CENSUS

Governments through the ages have consistently tried to keep tabs on what's going on in society and, from the Domesday Book in 1086 onwards, they've tried to compile facts and figures in as accurate a way as possible. (The Normans' method of accounting for each of their newly conquered subjects was to cut a notch on a stick, and then use the knife to stab them to death.) Traditionally, one simple, up-front method of gathering information has been the census. In the UK, the first proper, modern census took place in 1801, and one of the reasons for undertaking it was stated at the time, as follows:

> A census would indicate the Government's intention to promote the public good.

Nice to see that, even back in 1801, Government spin-doctors were on the ball.

A census relies for its accuracy on people telling the truth when filling in the form. As a result, it is an offence, punishable with a fine of up to £1,000, to either refuse to fill in a census form, or to enter details which you know to be incorrect. Which is interesting, because during the last UK census in 2001, some 390,000 'jokers' (let's just call them *that*, shall we?) decided to enter their religion as – wait for it – 'Jedi'. Oh, how we laughed. However, had the authorities decided to prosecute all of those people who thought it was so hilarious to claim fellowship with Yoda (or, rather, fellowship with Yoda to claim so hilarious it was), the public coffers would have been swollen by some £390 million-worth of fines. And a lot of people would have found that even *more* hilarious.

DATA COLLECTION

While the UK's next ten-yearly census will go ahead in 2011, the concept of the census, in terms of keeping tabs on people, is

The TV programme *Who Do You Think You Are?* has done a lot to improve the image of Government data collection in this country. Suddenly, people can see a valid reason for it, and are now turning excitedly to the online National Archives, desperate to track down some sort of a connection to William Caxton or Wellington or Vita Sackville-West. Or to make absolutely sure they're in no way related to Michael Winner. Mostly, though, everyone tends to come away having discovered only that their ancestors all had really grim jobs in mills or mines, or that the family line peters out in about 1830 (usually with a bloke called John who was a labourer from somewhere like Morpeth).

As regards the TV programme WDYTYA itself, how do the producers frame the rejection letter to someone whose family turns out to be, after a bit of research, mind-numbingly dull?

> Dear Mr Hoon,
> The good news is, we've managed to trace your family tree back several generations. The bad news is, no Hoon has ever done anything remotely interesting, with the exception of yourself, obviously. And even that, quite frankly, is stretching it a bit...'

now a bit passé. These days there's CCTV, number-plate readers, facial recognition systems, fingerprint and iris scanning, biometric information stored on chips, Facebook, reality TV shows, and so on – and the data from all these different sources can be instantly cross-referenced, or brought together and held on enormous databases. One of the few areas in which Britain leads the world is in the collection of data by the Government.

Another area where Britain leads the world is in the prompt loss of that same data by the Government. The ways Government departments have contrived to lose important data are many and varied: laptops containing confidential information have been left on trains, left in taxis, left in pubs, and put on eBay. Non-password-protected discs have gone missing in the post, and memory-sticks have been, er, forgotten about, and left lying around. You name it, and some idiot's done it, idiotically, due to their own idiocy –

including, in early 2009, Head of Counter-Terrorism Bob Quick strolling up Downing Street with a Top Secret document flapping in the breeze. The information on display related to imminent anti-terrorist raids, which then had to be hurriedly brought forward in case they'd been compromised.

Though, to be fair, the secret document was only visible to tabloid photographers with massive telephoto lenses, and who'd have thought there'd be any of those hanging about outside the Prime Minister's house in Downing Street?

Actually, this begs another question – who decided we needed a photo of Bob Quick getting out of a car, in the first place?

But, for whatever reason, the photo was taken, and Fleet Street editors were swift to lead the criticism, bleating, 'How irresponsible! What if this photo of secret information were to fall into the wrong hands?' Like, say, the hands of a Fleet Street editor, who would then responsibly splash it all over the front page.

Head of counter-terrorism Bob Quick:
An open-and-shut case… would have been a good idea

The ever-more rapacious acquisition – and the accompanying slapdash storage by the Government – of sometimes intensely personal information is a matter of considerable concern to civil liberties groups. Fair enough: it's their job, what else would they be doing (apart from booing at visiting Chinese politicians, and not buying certain types of fruit)? But it all goes back to Magna Carta, really (see above), which upholds your right to hear the 'case' against you, and to attempt to refute it. But if the 'case' against you is based on information held on a database somewhere, that may well have been gathered without your being aware of it, which you didn't even know was being retained, and the validity of which you've had no chance to challenge, then, basically, you're shafted, mate.

A good example of the seriousness of the issue is the mounting opposition to the long-term handling and storage of information on the British Government's ever-growing criminal DNA database. (That's a database of the DNA of criminals – and not a database of DNA *used* by criminals for some unspecified but no doubt nefarious purpose). This database is the largest in the world, containing five million DNA profiles, and has grown by forty per cent in the last two years. From the title, one would imagine it contains the DNA profiles of people who have committed a crime, and yes, it does. But it also contains the records of 850,000 people who have never been found guilty of committing any crime because they:

- were brought to trial but acquitted
- had their cases dropped, or
- were never even charged in the first place.

(It also contains the DNA profiles of 14 laboratory technicians, who accidentally sneezed over the rack of test tubes).

In December 2008, the European Court ruled that a blanket policy of indefinitely retaining the DNA of innocent people such as these (as is the practice in England and Wales) was illegal. In May 2009, the Government came back with its proposals. Effectively, they said 'All right, then – we won't keep the DNA profiles of innocent people indefinitely. We'll keep them for twelve years instead.' Not quite the response Liberty was hoping for. Back to court, then, chaps.

GOVERNMENT DATA-STORAGE SYSTEMS

TYPE	FOR	AGAINST

MEMORY STICK

Compact, highly portable, huge memory. Special *Star Wars* and *Doctor Who* versions available for the geeky 17-year-old junior clerks who are usually the ones entrusted with all this sensitive data. Some models even feature flashing lights — how cool is that?

Small enough to be easily lost, even by the Government's already impressive 'losing-things-easily' standards. Risks being thrown out by mistake, lost down the back of a sofa, or swallowed. Confusing and unfamiliar appearance to all employees over 40 — who frequently mistake it for a highlighter pen, or try to light their fags with it, before hurling it away in frustration.

DISK

Compact, highly portable, huge memory. If you hold one at the right angle, you can see lots of lovely rainbows. Ultra-reflective surface allows for more efficient interaction with laser system, and means you can also check your teeth after lunch for embarrassing spinach-flecks, etc. Great for make-up, too, ladies.

Easily damaged, as it looks far too much like a drinks coaster for its own good. Thin design means it is often lost among papers and accidentally thrown through open windows during office frisbee tournaments. Bright shiny appearance makes it a prime target for theft by magpie (117 cases reported last year, in Home Office alone).

LAPTOP COMPUTER

Fairly portable, huge memory, very wide range of features. Do you know what my best time is, for the 'expert' level on Minesweeper? — guess. Go on, have a guess. I'll tell you — 203 seconds. And there's 99 mines on that grid, so it's not easy.

So discreet a device, it's left on public transport on an almost daily basis. Also, despite claims as to versatility, its Games function patently lacks a 'replay' option, thereby depriving the user of the chance to relive the glory of his Minesweeper 'expert' personal best time. Which was 203 seconds. Disliked by more traditionally minded employees, who can mistake it for a ring binder, and are thus left confused and disappointed on opening it up.

– WHICH IS LEAST WORST?

TYPE	FOR	AGAINST

FLOPPY DISK

Nothing whatsoever. Apart from the fact you can use them to prop up a wobbly monitor.

Perversely, this is far too secure a system, as floppies are now so defunct, no one can read one. I had a report full of facts and figures on just how bad they are, which I'd got saved on a floppy – so we can kiss that goodbye. Also, they look like the sort of crackers that are served with the cheese at Heston Blumenthal's.

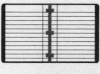

LOOSE-LEAF RING BINDER

Simple and lightweight. So much for the ministers, now how about the ring binder? No, seriously, you know where you are with one of these. Plus, they make that satisfying 'snapping' noise when you close them – you know, I could listen to that all day.

Have you ever trapped your finger when closing the rings in one of these things? You'd remember if you had. Very nasty. And the mess! Disliked by less traditionally minded employees, who can mistake it for a laptop, and are thus left confused and disappointed on opening it up.

PORTABLE MANUAL MEMO FILE

The most reliable and widely used system across all Government depart-ments. Idiot-proof, and almost minister-proof. And there's the additional benefit that, when your data-storage system gets lost, or goes disastrously wrong – which it will – you can literally 'wash your hands' of the whole affair.

Prone to 'spontaneous data-erasing leakage' – i.e. sweat, brought about by the sudden realisation that you've lost millions of items of sensitive information because you've left your memory stick, disk, laptop, floppy and ring binder on the bus.

The use of the latest technology to assemble criminal databases is supposed to minimise the risk of human error – you know the sort of thing: 'fleeing suicide bomber' = 'terrified Brazilian electrician'.

But proof of the fallibility of even the latest systems came in early in 2009, after new facial scanners were installed at Manchester Airport. In April, an expert in computer-based recognition systems from Glasgow University decided to run some tests of his own, replicating the same thirty per cent level of reliability at which the Manchester machines were reported to be operating. The results, to say the least, were disappointing: his tests showed that, at that level, the system was very bad at distinguishing between the faces scanned in – so bad, in fact, that it completely failed to differentiate between a photograph of Osama Bin Laden and one of Winona Ryder.

Spot the differences: Get five, and a job at Manchester Airport could be yours. Here's one to start you off – one of them's wearing a watch

One can only imagine the embarrassment it would cause to someone so emotionally vulnerable, were they to be mistaken for a common shoplifter and actress.

Now, most of us would accept that the likelihood of the 'World's Most Wanted Man' and the 'Woman Who Plays Captain Kirk's Mother In The Latest Star Trek Film' both happening to be going through passport control at Manchester Airport on the same day is fairly small. But it doesn't exactly fill one with confidence, does it?

RELIGION IN THE UK

According to Home Office figures, about seventy-two per cent of people in the UK consider themselves to be Christian. Quite a long way down comes the next biggest single religious grouping: Muslims, at just under three per cent of the population. Meanwhile, those who say they do not espouse any religion at all make up fifteen per cent.*

The Church of England is the established church in the UK. Except in Scotland, obviously, where the Church of Scotland, while not the established church, is, in many ways, the national church. And except in Wales, where the established church was the Church in Wales, but they disestablished themselves in the early twentieth century. (At this point, it's probably worth bringing up the word 'antidisestablishmentarianism' for no particular reason, other than it's one of the two ridiculously long words known by the sort of person who appears on TV quiz shows, the other being 'floccinaucinihilipilification', and that including both of them in the same sentence will, hopefully, give the people who have to typeset this book a real headache.) [*You'll have to try harder than that.* – Typesetter.]

So, one can safely state that the Church of England is the established church of, er, England. Which doesn't seem unreasonable. What this means in practice is that, in England, if you're taken to hospital in an emergency, the chances are the staff will pretty well automatically put 'C of E' on the paperwork. Unless you happen to

---

* *Interesting, then, that while a body exists which calls itself the 'Muslim Parliament of Great Britain', no 'Atheist Parliament of Great Britain' has ever existed or been suggested, despite the fact that they represent five times as many believers (or, rather, non-believers). Richard Dawkins missed a trick, there – but he's doing his best, God bless him.*

be wearing a burqa, a turban, or maybe a Catholic bishop's mitre. Or you happen to say something that gives them a reason not to, such as, 'Would you mind asking my wife to bring in my favourite black robe with the long sleeves, the golden sword the Chosen Ones presented me with, and that goat we were saving for a special occasion?'

But what does the phrase 'the established church' actually *mean*? In essence, it means that the Church of England is officially sanctioned and supported by the Government. Just as in Afghanistan, between 1996 and 2001, 'Taliban-ism' came to be the form of Islam officially sanctioned and supported by their government. In fairness to the C of E, they're nowhere near as fanatical as the Taliban. Although a bit more Afghan-style gusto might help bring a few punters back.

**The Archbishop of Canterbury and Mullah Omar:
On this evidence, it's clear that, if nothing else,
Anglicans have better cameras. But sillier eyebrows**

Because the C of E is the established church, when a bishop dies or retires, it's the Prime Minister of the day who gets to appoint his replacement – although the Queen, as Supreme Governor, is involved in formalising it. (Great title, that – 'Supreme Governor'. Wasn't there one of those in the first *Star Wars* film?) Of course, prime ministers don't have a completely free rein to just go right ahead and choose anyone they want. This is probably just as well,

In this country, one of the advantages of being the established church is that some of your bishops get to sit in the House of Lords. There are twenty-one of these 'Lords Spiritual', as they are known, and some are more high-profile than others. The Archbishops of Canterbury and York, and the Bishops of London, Durham and Winchester are those who generally attract the most media attention. One of the lesser known among the others, however, catapulted himself to prominence in December 2006, and, as a result, featured pretty heavily on that week's edition of HIGNFY. The Bishop of Southwark, who was making his way home from the Irish Embassy's Christmas party, for some reason decided that now was as good a time as any to climb into a stationary Mercedes and start throwing the children's toys he had found on the back seat out of the windows. When the owner, alerted to the goings-on by the going off of the car-alarm, asked the (under the circumstances) not-unreasonable question, 'What are you doing in my car?' the Bishop replied, 'I'm the Bishop of Southwark, it's what I do.'

The next day, the Bishop was photographed with a black eye, and the *Daily Telegraph* informed its readers that, as a result of the evening's shenanigans, 'His head was too swollen to wear his mitre.' Which, if you're a Bishop, is pretty bad news. One churchgoer at Southwark Cathedral told the papers, 'Anyone can make a mistake, and who are we to stand in judgement?' Fair enough. But it's not exactly 'standing in judgement' to find the whole thing well worth repeating, whenever bishops are mentioned.

Another of the time-honoured quirks of being a Church of England bishop is that, when you sign official documents, you get to use your Christian name, plus the abbreviated name, in Latin, of the place where you do your bishop-ing. If no Latin abbreviation exists for your city, the English name is used instead. So while you get some names with historic overtones – splendid, sonorous, uplifting names such as Rowan Cantuar (Canterbury) and David Sarum (Salisbury) – you also get bishops who are stuck with rather more prosaic-sounding Episcopal names, such as 'Kenneth Portsmouth'. Guess where he's Bishop of? And there have been other unfortunate name combinations over the years: until he retired in 2002, one bishop was obliged to sign himself 'Barry Bristol'. Which, as even he would have to admit, sounds more like a 1950s ventriloquist act. ('All things glight and gleautiful...)

otherwise back in Tony Blair's day we could well have seen Cliff Richard getting the nod as Bishop for somewhere or other.

What has been the Church of England's traditional role in the world? Obviously, a great deal of thought has gone into studying this question. But, when examining such matters, one cannot do better than to turn to the insightful body of research done by the writers Jimmy Perry and David Croft, and scrutinise the roles set out in their best-known and highly influential study of the workings of society: *Dad's Army*.

Dad's Army: Onward, Christian soldiers

Captain Mainwaring is a stickler for discipline, tends to believe he's right about absolutely everything, and tries to get everyone else to believe it, too – so he's obviously the Pope, then, isn't he? Whereas the pivotal role of Sergeant Wilson has clear similarities with that of the Archbishop of Canterbury. It's Wilson who always stands slightly to one side, murmuring, 'Do you really think that's wise?' when he reckons Mainwaring's gone too far; whenever relations between all the parties get heated, it's Wilson who tries to smooth things over, by manoeuvring them into some sort of compromise. Furthermore, domestically, Wilson constantly finds himself trying to negotiate the minefield of maintaining his relationship with the hard-line Mrs Pike (a traditionalist, perhaps, in many respects), while he takes care not to alienate her slightly effeminate son, Frank (a moderniser – in terms of scarf-wearing, certainly), towards whom Wilson displays a noticeable degree of tolerance, unlike Mainwaring, who merely regards him as a 'stupid boy'. It's a good part, though, the part of Wilson. It gets quite a lot of the laughs. And someone's got to play it, after all.

Who the other characters might represent is less clear. (Is Jones a Freemason? Is Godfrey a Quaker? Is Warden Hodges a Methodist? Is the Vicar… er… um… ah. Never mind.) In other words, this analogy hasn't really been thought through very thoroughly. Having said that, most people would see a fairly obvious, gloomy, Presbyterian parallel with the doom-laden mentality of Private Fraser.

On the whole, the Archbishop of Canterbury tries to keep out of the political arena. As a result, his public utterances pass largely unreported and, hence, unnoticed by the general public. Except, of course, on the occasions when they can be seized upon and construed by the media in such a way as to handily create or inflame controversy. When, in 2008, Dr Rowan Williams gave a lecture on the difficulty in resolving some of the conflicting aspects of Sharia Law and British Law, but suggested that, in some areas, a degree of accommodation would have to be found, he opened the papers next day to be faced with headlines such as 'ADOPT SHARIA LAW IN BRITAIN SAYS ARCHBISHOP OF CANTERBURY' and 'WILLIAMS: VICTORY FOR TERRORISTS'. So, in recent years, the dilemma faced by bishops in general, and the Archbishop of Canterbury in particular, has been: keep shtum, and be accused of being irrelevant, OR say what you think, and be accused of meddling. Tricky.

BRITISH CUSTOMS AND TRADITIONS

The Home Office guide to 'Life in the UK' tells us that, throughout the year, there are 'many festivals of music, art and culture, such as the Notting Hill Carnival and the Edinburgh Festival'. Couldn't they come up with a better list? For a start, there's that book thing at Hay-on-Wye, and… well, there must be lots of others. Surely.

Foreigners tend to go in for silly events like the festival in Buñol, near Barcelona, where people throw ripe tomatoes at each other.

Buñol Tomato Festival: Silly

This is not the British way: we favour more sensible occasions, such as rolling some Double Gloucester cheese down an incredibly steep hill and encouraging crowds of people to run after it. Much more dignified.

**Cooper's Hill Cheese Roll:
Not silly. Just really, really dangerous**

Obviously, were Buñol ever to be twinned with Cooper's Hill, the annual Cheese and Tomato Roll would become a huge tourist attraction. (Oh, come on – you were thinking it, too.)

HOLIDAYS

Throughout the year, there are special days that are celebrated across the land. Obviously, there's the big one, Christmas Day (25 December), which people celebrate by indulging in vast amounts of food and drink; Boxing Day (26 December), which people celebrate by indulging in vast amounts of food and drink; and New Year's Eve (31 December), which people celebrate by indulging in vast amounts of food and drink, before making resolutions to cut down on all their vast amounts of food and drink.

In an ever more secular world, Christmas has lost a lot of its religious significance. Mind you, it always was a bit of an odd concept – 'Hmm, how should we celebrate Jesus' birthday? I know, let's give *each other* some presents.' Nowadays, it's become a feeding-frenzy of mass consumerism, with people frantically racing around to buy stuff they'll be able to get seventy-five per cent cheaper in two days' time. In every town centre and shopping complex,* the scene at 5 p.m. on Christmas Eve looks like a cross between a plague of locusts and the Sack of Rome. ('Thank you, darling. A Pound-World own-brand roll-on deodorant-stick? Oh, you shouldn't have. No, really. You shouldn't have.') For most people, Christmas means travelling on trains so overcrowded it'd be illegal for livestock, eating lots of foods they don't actually like, and spending thirty-two minutes wrapping up a gift it'll then take somebody 0.6 seconds to *un*wrap. Any religious content which Christmas retains is so scant, it's a wonder God hasn't gone into a sulk, and crossed humanity off His son's birthday-card list.

---

* *'Shopping complex' means a centre or mall, and not that thing straight men have.*

CHRISTMAS – THE RISKS

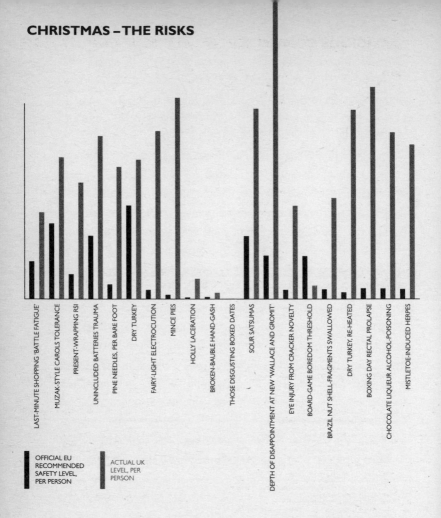

Legend:
- **OFFICIAL EU RECOMMENDED SAFETY LEVEL, PER PERSON**
- **ACTUAL UK LEVEL, PER PERSON**

Categories (left to right):
- LAST-MINUTE SHOPPING 'BATTLE FATIGUE'
- MUZAK-STYLE CAROLS TOLERANCE
- PRESENT-WRAPPING RSI
- UNINCLUDED BATTERIES TRAUMA
- PINE NEEDLES, PER BARE FOOT
- DRY TURKEY
- FAIRY-LIGHT ELECTROCUTION
- MINCE PIES
- HOLLY LACERATION
- BROKEN-BAUBLE HAND-GASH
- THOSE DISGUSTING BOXED DATES
- SOUR SATSUMAS
- DEPTH OF DISAPPOINTMENT AT NEW 'WALLACE AND GROMIT'
- EYE INJURY FROM CRACKER NOVELTY
- BOARD-GAME BOREDOM THRESHOLD
- BRAZIL NUT SHELL-FRAGMENTS SWALLOWED
- DRY TURKEY, RE-HEATED
- BOXING DAY RECTAL PROLAPSE
- CHOCOLATE LIQUEUR ALCOHOL-POISONING
- MISTLETOE-INDUCED HERPES

Easter (no idea, any Sunday between 22 March and 25 April; they keep moving it, for some reason) is another religious festival that isn't religious any more (see above). Briefly, it's exactly like Christmas, except the turkey is replaced by chocolate eggs and the weather's not as good. Depressingly, in a survey in March 2005, only forty-eight per cent of the adults questioned knew why Easter was celebrated – proof, if it were needed, that eating chocolate makes you stupid.

RELIGIOUS CONVICTION vs DELICIOUS CONFECTION

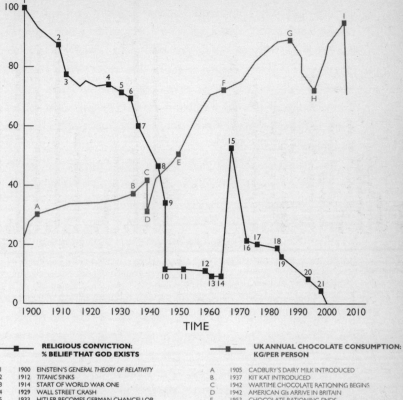

	RELIGIOUS CONVICTION: % BELIEF THAT GOD EXISTS			UK ANNUAL CHOCOLATE CONSUMPTION: KG/PER PERSON

I	1900	EINSTEIN'S *GENERAL THEORY OF RELATIVITY*	A	1905	CADBURY'S DAIRY MILK INTRODUCED
2	1912	*TITANIC* SINKS	B	1937	KIT KAT INTRODUCED
3	1914	START OF WORLD WAR ONE	C	1942	WARTIME CHOCOLATE RATIONING BEGINS
4	1929	WALL STREET CRASH	D	1942	AMERICAN GIs ARRIVE IN BRITAIN
5	1933	HITLER BECOMES GERMAN CHANCELLOR	E	1953	CHOCOLATE RATIONING ENDS
6	1936	CHARLIE CHAPLIN CONTINUES TO MAKE FILMS	F	1967	MICK JAGGER/MARIANNE FAITHFULL RUMOUR STARTS
7	1939	START OF WORLD WAR TWO	G	1990	MARATHON CHANGES ITS NAME TO SNICKERS
8	1945	US DROPS ATOM BOMBS ON HIROSHIMA AND NAGASAKI	H	1999	KIT KAT CHUNKY INTRODUCED
9	1948	NOEL EDMONDS BORN	I	2009	MP HAZEL BLEARS REVEALED TO BE A FAN OF KIT KAT CHUNKY
10	1948	'BIG BANG' THEORY PUBLISHED			
11	1954	FIRST APPEARANCE OF HUMAN FACES IN *TOM AND JERRY*			
12	1961	BERLIN WALL ERECTED			
13	1963	PRESIDENT J F KENNEDY ASSASSINATED			
14	1966	ENGLAND WINS WORLD CUP			
15	1970	ENGLAND DOESN'T WIN WORLD CUP			
16	1975	COACH BRAKES WORK PERFECTLY THROUGHOUT ENTIRE SWISS LEG OF BAY CITY ROLLERS TOUR			
17	1979	MARGARET THATCHER BECOMES PRIME MINISTER			
18	1986	CHERNOBYL NUCLEAR REACTOR MELTDOWN			
19	1987	GARY FUCKING RHODES			
20	1997	DIANA, PRINCESS OF WALES DIES			
21	2001	BBC BROADCASTS FIRST EPISODE OF *TWO PINTS OF LAGER AND A PACKET OF CRISPS*			

From this information, it is obvious that the decline in religious belief would have been reversed, if only confectioners in 1946 had been innovative enough to bring out a chocolate figure of Jesus.

Christmas, Easter and a couple of other obscure occasions are also marked by being bank holidays. When it comes to these, no one really knows what's going on – is it called a bank holiday because it was *only* the banks that used to be closed? Or because everything used to be closed, *including* the banks? What happens when the bank has had to be bailed out, and is now part-owned by the taxpayer? It's all academic, really, because most places just stay open nowadays. And you can always get cashback at the supermarket, if you like.

For many people, though, a bank holiday means they get to have a day off work, so they can go out and end up blind drunk, instead. Then, next day, they get to have a day off work.

Another 'special' occasion is Valentine's Day (14 February), which is traditionally marked by the newspapers printing pointless, nauseating messages from people calling themselves things like 'Snuffly Bunny' to people calling themselves things like 'The Hairy Bear'. They spout vomit-inducing drivel to each other along the lines of, 'Boo-hoo, sniff, sniff – Captain Bouncy loses his twinkle when Little Miss Trampolina isn't around for fluffy snuggles and huggery.' Quite why otherwise perfectly normal people should feel the need to lapse into this form of twee, stomach-churning baby-talk for one day a year remains something of a mystery.

A recent welcome (or is it?) addition to the calendar of festivities is the hugely entertaining (or is it?) 'trick-or-treating' that children indulge in around Hallowe'en (31 October). This amounts to little more than demanding money with menaces, an activity for which people used to get put away in the East End of the 1960s – how times have changed. Hallowe'en is essentially an American import: no one in Britain ever used to bother to mark the day, because the much more exciting Fifth of November (er, 5 November) was coming up, shortly afterwards.

A thoroughly English tradition, Bonfire Night recalls the occasion in 1605 when the Catholic Guy Fawkes and his fellow conspirators tried and failed to blow up Parliament, with the Protestant King inside. Fireworks are let off, food is cooked outdoors, and effigies of Fawkes are made and burned. All over the country, happy, laughing children celebrate the fact that, after being caught and then tortured for several days, Fawkes was sentenced, along with the other plotters, to be:

> ... hanged by the Necks, then cut down alive, their Privy-Members cut off, and their Bowels taken out to be burned before their Faces, their Heads to be severed from their Bodies, and their Bodies divided into four parts, to be disposed of as the King should think fit.

Anyway, have another sausage.

Nowadays, at large events organised locally, it has become a tradition for whoever the public has hated most during the course of the year to be set on top of the bonfire and burned. So this year, as the crowd contentedly warm themselves from a safe distance, listen out for the cheering as the local ex-MP goes up in flames. Or their effigy. Or an effigy of their duck island.

PART FOUR

HOW THE UK IS GOVERNED

DECISION-MAKING ABILITIES OF THE BRITISH PUBLIC

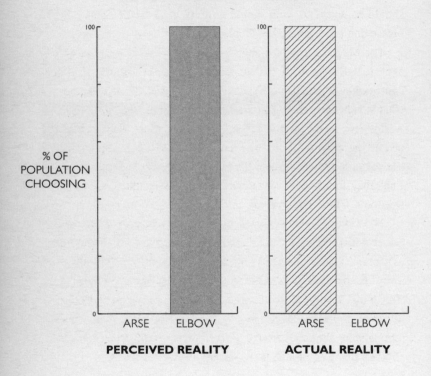

THE BRITISH CONSTITUTION

This is likely to be a short section, because there isn't one. At least, there isn't a *written* constitution. Many people think there should be, but if so, who should write it? And for heaven's sake, please don't everybody say Stephen Fry.

The Magna Carta (see above) is probably the closest we ever came to it. But for many British people, the idea of having a written constitution is anathema. Or at least it would be, if anyone knew what 'anathema' meant. The whole issue can be reduced to a certain world view: a constitution defines what is allowed, whereas many people prefer to think that *not* having a constitution implies that *everything*'s allowed, except the things which the law says aren't. This, they fondly believe, safeguards our rights and fundamental freedoms. Close, but no cigar.

The catch is, not having a constitution also means that the Government deems itself free to erect as many CCTV cameras as it can afford, collect as much data about its citizens on as many databases as it likes (see above), and generally exercise its 'freedoms' too, because there is no fundamental constitutional bar to it doing so. Some people say it's a case of swings and roundabouts, though there are, in fact, plans for all other items of children's play equipment to be covered by CCTV as well.

THE MONARCHY

The Queen is the Head of State of the United Kingdom. (Get over it, Charles. If it happens, it happens.) It's a constitutional monarchy, which in simple terms means that the Monarch appoints the Government, and the Government then rules the country. Just as with the appointment of a bishop (see above), the Queen is not free to appoint any old person she happens to take a shine to, to run the country: she has to go with the leader of the party that wins the most seats in a general election. Now, it might be that the Queen doesn't happen to particularly like the person concerned. Suppose, for instance, that the Queen thought that the leader of one of the main parties was bad-tempered, psychologically flawed, charmless, chippy and Scottish. She might also regard one of the other party leaders as an oily, lightweight, smug, baby-faced careerist, and forget about the third one completely. Who knows? Her Majesty is too discreet ever to let such things show. But in the end, it makes no difference: she just appoints the Prime Minister, she doesn't get to choose who it is. She gets so frustrated by this, she often has to go and count her dominions, until she's calmed down a bit.

One of the monarch's traditional duties every year is to attend the State Opening of Parliament. (She has to, she's got the only key.) It's one of those occasions that the rest of the world thinks is marvellous, but which, in Britain, divides opinion: some people find it charmingly and reassuringly old-fashioned, while others regard it as encapsulating all that's wrong with the way the country is still governed in the modern age. The Queen's main duty at the State Opening is to read out the forthcoming legislative programme proposed by the Government, whether she agrees with it or not (while trying to keep a straight face throughout).

THE PRIME MINISTER

After the Germans took over the Monarchy (in other words, after the accession to the throne of George I following the death of Queen Anne) the running of the country came increasingly to be

Since it comes round at least once a year, the Queen's Speech at the State Opening has often been a topic for discussion on HIGNFY. Paul Merton has speculated about how tempting it must be for the Queen to just read the whole thing out in a silly voice one year, simply because she can.

Ian Hislop has compared the role of the Queen at the State Opening to that of the guest host on HIGNFY: he sometimes accuses the host of just reading out whatever's put in front of them by the writers, regardless of whether they agree with it or find it funny. This is not really a fair comparison, though – in reality, the producers always politely invite the guest hosts to express an opinion on the material they've been given. Only once they've done that are they politely invited to keep those opinions to themselves because it's nearly four o'clock, the host's script really needed to go to autocue about half an hour ago, and there really isn't time for all this, OK?

undertaken by a group of ministers in Parliament. Over time, the position of 'Prime Minister' evolved: Sir Robert Walpole in the 1720s is regarded as the first man to hold the position. Walpole was able to exercise control over the Government because he held the office of 'First Lord Of The Treasury', and the same is true of the Prime Minister today: he or she too holds the official position of 'First Lord of The Treasury'. And indeed if you look closely at the letterbox on the door of Number 10 Downing Street, you can see that title is engraved in the brass.

The Chancellor of the Exchequer is thus technically the *Second* Lord of the Treasury, and so theoretically subordinate in all decisions regarding Treasury matters to the First Lord, although it would have taken a brave man to remind Gordon Brown of that fact when he was Chancellor. (He's quite prepared to agree with it now that he's Prime Minister.)

Alistair Darling: Very much the Second Lord of the Treasury

Traditionally, the Prime Minister lives at Number 10 Downing Street, while the Chancellor lives at Number 11. During Tony Blair's premiership however, it was Gordon Brown, as Chancellor, who actually lived at Number 10, while Blair himself, for reasons of space given his expanding family at the time, lived at Number 11. Which perhaps explains the strange hold Gordon Brown exercised over Blair during the latter years: he'd been reading his post.

THE POSITION OF DEPUTY PRIME MINISTER

The position of Deputy Prime Minister doesn't really exist. It was created by the coalition Government during the Second World War, when the office was given to Clement Attlee to enable Churchill to concentrate on running the war. Interestingly, the second holder of the post was Herbert Morrison, grandfather of Peter Mandelson, and it's not beyond the bounds of possibility that Mandelson still has ambitions to emulate his grandfather in this respect. After all, he succeeded in getting himself put in charge of the (disastrous)

Millennium Dome project, a role parallel to his grandfather's as coordinator of the Festival of Britain some fifty years before. The position of Deputy PM was revived in the 1980s at the whim of Prime Minister Margaret Thatcher, a woman well known for her whim of iron. She bestowed it upon William Whitelaw, who was elevated to the peerage in 1983 (not without difficulty, as he was a big lad). Since there is no real constitutional background to the title, there would appear to be no constitutional bar to the Deputy Prime Minister being in the Lords. It would be a foolish man who would bet against the possibility of Lord Mandelson getting Gordon Brown in some sort of political arm-lock at some stage in the future and making a move on the vacant title.

The title of Deputy PM was again revived by the Blair Government on coming to power in 1997 and awarded to John Prescott, which some people took as unmistakable confirmation that it was never really meant to be taken seriously as a peacetime title in the first place. The holder of the post of Deputy PM has various official duties, although it's probably fair to say that throughout the entire time John Prescott held the office no one seemed able to pinpoint precisely what they were. The one duty it was possible to point to was that of standing in at Prime Minister's Questions in the House of Commons whenever Tony Blair was having a holiday at Sir Cliff Richard's Barbados villa, which seemed to happen quite a lot.* Nevertheless, large sums of public money were deemed necessary to run the DPM's office – those chest freezers and gas-fired barbecue sets don't come cheap. Plus, you have to pay the cleaning staff extra whenever you and your secretary need the tops

---

* *Gordon Brown chooses not to spend time at Cliff Richard's Barbados villa. On the other hand, perhaps Sir Cliff Richard chooses not to invite Gordon Brown to spend time at his Barbados villa. You don't have to know Gordon Brown personally to imagine why that might be the case.*

of your desks hosed down. Under Gordon Brown, there is no Deputy Prime Minister (the very *idea* of Gordon allowing someone to hold a title like that unless it was absolutely unavoidable…). However, the country does rather seem to muddle along quite happily without one, and with considerably less outlay from the public purse.

Interestingly, by a tradition that dates back at least eight years, the holder of the office of Deputy Prime Minister is, under English Law, the only person allowed to punch someone in the face with impunity, apart from the reigning monarch and his consort.[*]

RECENT PRIME MINISTERS

Margaret Thatcher came to power in 1979, and remained in office until 1990. This is almost literally true, as she hardly ever left her office, famously claiming to need only four hours sleep a night. And it didn't even need to be in a proper bed – all she required was a small patch of deconsecrated soil from her native land, and some tasty beetles.

Thatcher: On a sledge

---

[*] *The current Queen has so far chosen not to exercise this right, having witnessed a distressing incident at Sandringham over Christmas 1951 when Queen Elizabeth the Queen Mother, then the wife of King George VI, split the lip of the Archbishop of York after a particularly frustrating game of Rummy.*

Her economic policies were based around encouraging a free-market economy but retaining strict control of the money supply in order to maintain a stranglehold on inflation – a political legacy that still continues in the UK today. Or at least it would have done had not Gordon Brown failed, as Chancellor, to put any money aside for a rainy day during the good years, despite banging on and on about 'prudence' all the time. And had he not, as Prime Minister, presided over the total collapse of the UK economy and found himself forced to use massive amounts of taxpayers' money to bail out the failing UK banks. And had he not, in doing so, simply run out of money and been forced to just start printing more in order to try and get the economy moving again – never mind what that does to confidence in the currency and inflation in the longer term, and bugger the lessons to be learned from what happened when they tried that in Germany in the 1930s. Margaret Thatcher must be spinning in her grave (please check if she is still alive before this book goes to print).

John Major succeeded Margaret Thatcher. (A rare example, there, of the words 'John', 'Major' and 'succeeded' in the same sentence.) Here's a picture of him in a strange hat:

Major: In a strange hat

If he is remembered at all, it is for one remarkable achievement – managing to keep under his hat (possibly that one) the fact that, whilst he was a Government Whip under Margaret Thatcher, and without his wife Norma ever finding out, he spent four years shagging the rather blowsy Edwina Currie, a member of his Cabinet during the 1990s.

Edwina Currie: In fairly typical pose, it transpires – make up your own 'Cabinet bike' jokes

Currie didn't tell anyone about the affair until many years later (2002) and even then only when she was under a truly astonishing amount of pressure (to come up with something that would help sell her soon-to-be-released diaries). In the diaries she revealed: 'I taught [Major] to stretch out, keep stretching, go through barriers, push and push oneself, find oneself out in the stratosphere, float out there with your lover, together with laughter drifting past the stars.' How lovely that sounds.

After the Major era, the Conservatives lost power, and Tony Blair took office with a massive parliamentary majority. The Labour Party rebranded itself as 'New Labour' to distinguish itself from 'Old Labour', although in reality the two factions co-existed. On the 'New Labour' side were such figures as Tony Blair, Gordon Brown, Peter Mandelson, Robin Cook, Alan Milburn, Geoff Hoon and Alastair Campbell, while 'Old Labour' was represented by, er, John Prescott. Blair's masterstroke was to wave the Prime Ministerial wand and bestow upon John Prescott the title of Deputy Prime Minister (see above). By doing that he made sure that 'Old Labour' felt it had not just a voice in Cabinet, but a grumpy, sweary, shouty northern voice at that. Placated by the presence of Prescott at the 'top table', what was left of 'Old Labour' appeared to lose its way somewhat on the socialist agenda it professed to espouse and seemed happy to just let Blair get on and do more or less whatever he wanted for about 11 years. So the plan worked a treat, then, eh, Tony?

But the Conservatives weren't idle during the Blair years. Oh, sorry – actually, yes, they were. They did absolutely nothing at all under three successive leaders: William Hague, the other bald one I can't even be bothered googling, and Michael Howard.

**This man was the leader of Her Majesty's Opposition.
No, really, he was**

It was only when David Cameron took over that their fortunes began to revive. Cameron wowed everyone at the Conservative Party Conference the year he took over by making a speech without notes, something John Prescott might as well have been doing for the last forty years, for all the difference his having notes made to the intelligibility of the end product. Unlike Prescott, Cameron took a radical approach to speechmaking and included a few verbs along the way and, as a result, his speech made sense. In the Press Gallery, despite it being just after lunch, they spotted this and were instantly won over.

Prescott's use and abuse of language was legendary, and provided much innocent and not-so-innocent amusement for his many fans in the media. Here, for the record, is a sample – a direct quote, as reported in the newspapers and read out by Jeremy Clarkson who was hosting *Have I Got News for You* the week it happened:

> Look I've got my old pledge card a bit battered and crumpled, we said we'd provide more turches churches teachers and we have. I can remember when people used to say the Japanese are better than us, the Germans are better than us, the French are better than us well it's great to be able to say we're better than them. I think Mr Kennedy well we all congratulate on his baby and the Tories are you remembering what I'm remembering boom and bust negative equity, remember Mr Howard, I mean are you thinking what I'm thinking I'm remembering, it's all a bit wonky isn't it?

Incidentally, the late Linda Smith once said of him: 'I don't think language is his first language.'

Eventually, Tony Blair's fingers were prised off the levers of power. A rising tide of bad stuff had been swirling around him for some time. Nothing big, really – just the unpopularity of the Iraq war generally, that business about the alleged sexing-up of information relating to Iraq's weapons capability and the 'dodgy dossier', the suicide of Government scientist Dr David Kelly, the Hutton Inquiry into the affair, the fact that no Weapons of Mass Destruction were ever found in Iraq, and the whole 'Cash For Honours' scandal (see below). Hardly anything at all, in fact.

And then, just when people thought things couldn't get any worse, Gordon Brown took over, and the entire world economy collapsed. Probably just a coincidence, though.

PARLIAMENT

Prior to the reforms pushed through by the Labour Government at the end of the last century, there had been one UK Parliament for hundreds of years, to which members were elected from all over the United Kingdom. Now, after many years of campaigning, Scotland has its own Parliament, and Wales and Northern Ireland have their own Assemblies. England, apparently, couldn't be arsed to join in.

This situation does not affect England unduly however. The differences are, in practice, few and minor: for example English students have to run up debts of many thousands of pounds to pay for their tuition fees while at university, whereas Scottish students don't. English patients have to pay a prescription charge of £7.20 per item for their medicines as prescribed by their doctors, some patients with serious illnesses being prescribed four or five items at a time, whereas Welsh patients don't and Scottish patients soon won't. Oh, and English pensioners often have to sell their houses to pay accommodation fees when they need to go into a nursing home whereas Scottish pensioners don't.

So, it's only in relatively unimportant areas like education, lifelong health and the right to a comfortable old age that the difference between life in England and life in the rest of the United Kingdom shows up. Although it's interesting to note that over the last thirty years or so, under the particular funding rules in force in the UK, every Scottish person has received something in the region of £1,500 more in public spending on average than their English counterparts (according to 2007 figures). However, the discrepancies in Scottish funding, which are quite noticeable compared with some of the English regions, were once described by Tony Blair as 'a small price to pay to keep the UK together'. And anyway it's all fine with the English, who don't appear to have let the inequality bother them. Otherwise, surely someone would have taken the matter up with either the current Prime Minister (a Scot), the previous Prime Minister (born in Scotland), the current Chancellor of the Exchequer (a Scot), or the previous Chancellor of the Exchequer (a Scot).

THE COMMONS AND THE LORDS

Parliament is divided into two houses: the Lords and the Commons. The Home Office 'Life in the UK' handbook states: 'Nowadays, the Prime Minister and almost all the members of the Cabinet are members of the House of Commons.' However, that fails to take into account the tendency amongst recent Prime Ministers simply to decide who they think they'd like for a particular ministerial job, nominate them for a peerage, and so bring them into the Government the easy way. The advantage of this system is that it means the person concerned doesn't ever have to do anything so inconvenient as actually having to stand for election, dear me, no. And it also means that the person is never put in the uncomfortable position of having to justify decisions they or their department have taken, by getting up and speaking in the bear-pit atmosphere of the House of Commons, in front of other members (who, unlike them, hold a democratic mandate to be there). Instead, they can make quiet, low-key, gentlemanly statements in the rather more genteel setting of the Lords – so much more agreeable, one finds. (And with the added bonus that at least half their audience will be asleep on their benches, and won't hear their speech, and the other half will barely hear it through all the snoring).

This handy 'House of Lords card' can be played on other occasions, too. If as PM, due to a lack of available talent, you find yourself in the slightly embarrassing position of ending up having to bring back into the Cabinet someone who's a bit unpopular with the public, and so would probably never get a Commons seat again – someone, say, who has had to resign on no fewer than *two* previous occasions for various reasons – easy: just make them a Lord. Mentioning no Mandelsons.

THE CABINET – WHO DOES WHAT?

Officially, the Cabinet is a formal body composed of the most senior Government ministers – and not, as you might increasingly believe, a feckless shower of craven, self-serving buffoons who are clearly well out of their depth, and the sort of people you wouldn't trust to run a bath, let alone the country.

Cabinet ministers are chosen by the Prime Minister, who assesses each individual's particular talents and skills in relevant areas, before appointing them to a ministerial post for which they are entirely unsuitable. This can be proven by the following formula:

Alistair Darling as Chancellor + greatest financial crisis ever = coincidence?

Having blundered along with his 'team' of misfits, the PM might, for a number of reasons, see fit to have a Cabinet reshuffle. This gives him the chance to shake things up, to refresh Government policy, and to appoint completely different people to ministerial posts for which they are entirely unsuitable.

Or at least, that's what used to happen. In June 2009, the MPs' expenses scandal led to a rash of ministerial resignations. (You'd think they'd be able to get a tube of ointment for that – and then claim for six of them.) A desperately beleaguered Gordon Brown was forced to attempt a reshuffle, but he then had to struggle with a couple of new difficulties (which, bearing in mind how many difficulties he'd already struggled with, is no mean feat).

Some Cabinet ministers, Darling among them, simply refused to switch to other posts, and were determined to stick to their guns. (Guns – now there's an idea.) The main problem, though, was that so many ministers had stepped down that Gordon, to extend the 'shuffle' analogy, wasn't dealing with a full pack. Many of the cards were missing, and all he had left was a couple of jokers. The PM wanted to 'twist', but the Chancellor was determined to 'stick'. The whole house of cards looked ready to collapse, much as this contorted metaphor already has. On seeing the reshuffled Cabinet that Brown eventually ended up with, however, one thing became obvious: the immediate need for an instant reshuffle.

But how exactly does the Cabinet work? The following information should clear up a lot of questions, as well as fill up a bit of space.

FIRST SECRETARY OF STATE
LORD PRESIDENT OF THE COUNCIL
LORD CHANCELLOR
CHANCELLOR OF THE DUCHY OF LANCASTER
PAYMASTER GENERAL
SECRETARY OF STATE FOR BUSINESS, INNOVATION, AND SKILLS
Probably all Peter Mandelson.

CHANCELLOR OF THE EXCHEQUER
The financial 'brains' of the outfit. Regarded as the Number Two job in Government after the
PM, but just ask Gordon which one he was happier doing. Tradition dictates that the
Chancellor is obliged to use Denis Healey's old prototype calculator from 1975 to work out
all the necessary calculations. Not many people know that this battered device is what's kept
inside that mysterious little red box which Chancellors are always pictured holding aloft,
placed alongside their packed lunch, a clean pair of underpants, and a cyanide capsule.

SECRETARY OF STATE FOR CHILDREN, SCHOOLS AND FAMILIES
Proof that it's not just education that's been dumbed down, but also
the title of the minister responsible for it. And since when did 'Children'
need a minister? – a quick slap round the back of the legs would be
more like it.

SECRETARY OF STATE FOR HEALTH
Tends to have best BUPA package of anyone in
Parliament. This is not a coincidence.

SECRETARY OF STATE FOR
TRANSPORT
Tends to have best fleet of flashy private
cars of anyone in Parliament. This is not
a coincidence.

SECRETARY OF STATE FOR
CULTURE, MEDIA AND SPORT
Polite term for a front-bench-potato.

SECRETARY OF STATE FOR SCOTLAND
Jock-jockey.

SECRETARY OF STATE FOR WALES
Chief of Taff.

LORD PRIVY SEAL
Toff who keeps marine
mammals in his loo.

SECRETARY OF STATE FOR THE ENVIRONMENT, FOOD AND RURAL AFFAIRS
Tidies the office, sorts out the tea and biscuits, and, er, does something rural.

PRIME MINISTER, AND FIRST LORD OF THE TREASURY

Head honcho – if, by 'honcho', you mean 'culprit'. Apparently, a new prerequisite for the role is the ability to smile inanely for no reason – Blair could, Brown demonstrably and most definitely can't. When he smiles, it looks like someone's suddenly inserted an electrode into his brain. Maybe they have, and that's what it takes to get him to loosen up. The Prime Minister also has the ultimate power to choose who should, or shouldn't, be in the Cabinet – unless, of course, he's an introspective ditherer who can't make a simple decision. Or unless he's not.

SECRETARY OF STATE FOR THE HOME DEPARTMENT

Not so much a Cabinet seat, more of an ejector seat. In recent years, there seem to have been as many home secretaries as MPs have homes. And secretaries.

SECRETARY OF STATE FOR FOREIGN AND COMMONWEALTH AFFAIRS

A post usually held by the only member of the Cabinet who 'can' 'speak' 'French'. Gets to sit nearest to the office globe – which, like most things in Cabinet, is subjected to a lot of spin. Main responsibility is to give the impression that the UK is as powerful as it used to be. Fails.

SECRETARY OF STATE FOR DEFENCE

Main responsibility is to give the impression that the UK is as powerful as it used to be. Fails miserably.

MINISTER FOR WOMEN AND EQUALITY

Token post, to keep the little ladies happy.

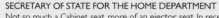

KEY

1 TOOTH MARKS ON CARPET (M. THATCHER)
2 OLD GRAFFITI (J. MAJOR)
3 UNPLEASANT CARPET STAIN (N. LAMONT)
4 GUIDE-DOG SCRATCHES (D. BLUNKETT)
5 STAIN, POSSIBLY CHICKEN DHANSAK (J. PRESCOTT)

SECRETARY OF STATE FOR INTERNATIONAL DEVELOPMENT

This is just taking the piss, now.

SECRETARY OF STATE FOR ENERGY AND CLIMATE CHANGE

Pass.

SECRETARY OF STATE FOR NORTHERN IRELAND

For a long time, ministers who held this post were always nervous. Then they stopped being nervous for a while. Now, they're suddenly nervous again.

SECRETARY OF STATE FOR COMMUNITIES AND LOCAL GOVERNMENT

Nope.

SECRETARY OF STATE FOR WORK AND PENSIONS

Sorry, no idea.

SECRETARY OF STATE FOR JUSTICE

Whatsisname, you know, the one used to wear glasses. Duties include responsibility for the prison system – a system which many MPs would be much more familiar with the internal workings of, if there was any justice (which the Justice Minister makes sure there isn't).

THE HOUSE OF LORDS AND
THE 'CASH FOR HONOURS' SCANDAL

There are, of course, other ways of getting into the House of Lords (and not just by logging on to www.fathersforjustice.co.uk/annoyingstunts/floor-plans). Distinguished people in particular fields have, since the 1950s, been eligible for life peerages, and the Prime Minister of the day is entitled to nominate people for the upper house. As part of New Labour's 1997 election manifesto, Tony Blair began to remove more and more hereditary peers from the House of Lords and nominate increasing numbers of life peers. It would have made a total nonsense of Blair's pledge that his administration would be 'whiter than white' if life peerages had been handed out in return for favours to New Labour, and thank goodness that never happened. No – what became known as the 'Cash for Honours' scandal was in fact a set of astonishing and unfortunate coincidences which only made the whole system *appear* to be a rotting pile of shite.

Tony Blair always wanted to see his party freed from the traditional financial stranglehold of Trade Unions. So big donations were prised out of wealthy businessmen and others by Blair and his tennis partner and party 'money-man'* Lord Levy. Some of these donations, the larger ones mainly, were made in the form of loans at favourable rates of interest. Because of a loophole in the guidelines (there's always a loophole if you throw enough money at the problem), donations above a certain level had to be declared, whereas loans didn't – so the identities of the lenders could be kept secret. Entirely coincidentally, some of the donors/lenders had been given honours and peerages or been recommended for them.

Thanks to a few MPs suggesting that something dodgy was going on, the police were called in to investigate whether there was a causal

---

* *'Tennis partner' is not an official Cabinet position. Yet.*

link between the giving of a donation or the making of a loan and the receipt of a peerage, or whether it was all just an innocent coincidence. The police interviewed Lord Levy and Blair several times (the first time a serving Prime Minister had ever been quizzed by the police). In the end, the Crown Prosecution Service decided that there was insufficient evidence to prosecute anyone. And why wouldn't they? Let's say that every time someone walks towards a pair of sliding doors at a supermarket, the doors open of their own accord; even if this happens a hundred times in a row, there is no reason to suppose that there is any causal link between the person moving towards the sliding doors and the doors opening. And to do so would be to cast an outrageous slur on the reputation of the sliding doors.

Statisticians are cautious chaps, and good at being dispassionate about things. They are always wary of attributing causal links to two sets of collected data, however much in parallel they seem to run. (The sets of data, that is, not the statisticians – the statisticians couldn't really run in parallel, as they tend to be desk-bound and not very sporty). What they prefer to say in such cases is that they have established an 'observable correlation' between two variables. So why not have a go at plotting a graph with 'Name Put Forward For Ennoblement Under Prime Minister Tony Blair' on one axis and 'Large Donation/Loan Made To The Labour Party Under Prime Minister Tony Blair' on the other. See if it's possible to establish an 'observable correlation'.

THE HOUSE OF COMMONS AND THE MEMBERS' ALLOWANCES SCANDAL

Members of the House of Commons are paid a salary – currently around £65,000 a year. In addition, they are (or perhaps by the time this book appears, *were*) entitled to claim various allowances. The House of Commons 'Green Book' sets out the rules covering claims like this, a copy of which is given to all MPs. It's important to bear in mind (because many of them seem not to have done) that the rules state quite clearly:

> Expenditure for which reimbursement is claimed …
> should be wholly, exclusively and necessarily incurred for
> the performance of a member's parliamentary duties.

In 2009, relentless media interest began to focus on the issue of MPs' allowances. The whole matter had been brought to a head when applications were made under freedom-of-information legislation to view the details of the claims. This was on the basis that, since MPs' salaries and allowances are paid out of public money, they should be available for scrutiny. MPs were given the chance to vote on whether the details should be exempted from the provisions of the Freedom of Information Act and therefore kept secret – and they voted to keep them secret. The then Speaker of the House of Commons spent nearly four years and several hundred thousand pounds battling to keep the details of MPs' allowances claims to themselves. And as soon as the details started to emerge, it became pretty obvious why there had been such a reluctance to share the information with the public.

In 2009, the full details of the allowances MPs had been claiming were finally scheduled for release in the summer, when governments traditionally sneak out anything that might prove to be embarrassing for them – Parliament is generally in recess and journalists are often away, so it's usually a good time to 'bury bad news' (© Jo Moore 2001).

Over several weeks in March and April, odd snippets of information dribbled out – such as Home Secretary Jacqui Smith designating her sister's house in London, where she had a room, as her principal residence, while her husband and family stayed in her secondary residence (that'll be the large family home in the constituency, then). In addition, it turned out that her husband, who also receives a taxpayer-funded salary to act as her assistant, had absent-mindedly claimed under her MP's allowances for the cost of viewing pornographic films, a detail which the tabloids covered in their traditionally sensitive manner.

It had been known for a while that a great deal more of this detailed information might be available – the Jacqui Smith stuff was just a 'taster'. A copy of the MPs' claims had somehow been

JOHN 'TWO LAVS' PRESCOTT

Some of the content of the claims made for entertaining reading. We now know that in December 2004 John Prescott suffered an incident resulting in trashed-toilet-seat trauma. Luckily, the taxpayer was on hand (though, mercifully, not literally) and leapt to the rescue, generously funding its fixing. Then, worryingly, less than two short years later, the then Deputy Prime Minister appears to have experienced a further lavatory-linked lapse of an unspecified nature, and once again taxpayers magnanimously opened up their wallets and purses and chipped in to enable the necessary remedial work to be carried out on his seat. This is all rather alarming: keen Prescott watchers can't have failed to notice that, by now, more than two years have elapsed since his last khazi-connected catastrophe. It's a bit like waiting for the next tsunami: it can surely only be a matter of time. Let no one say they haven't been warned.

leaked or stolen and was being touted around the newspapers. In early May, the *Daily Telegraph* got access to the full details and started publishing them. (The paper was, however, unwilling to either confirm or deny that money had changed hands; they also found themselves unwilling to confirm or deny the precise religious affiliation of the Pope, and any topographical information regarding the toilet habits of bears.)

There were other more serious issues raised when the claims were made public. For instance, it turned out that many MPs had changed the designation of their two homes with the authorities (usually once or twice, but sometimes as many as six times), a process that became known as 'flipping'. (This is possibly a reference to the 1960s TV dolphin, Flipper, who infamously fiddled his taxes by claiming expenses on two dolphinaria at the same time.) The advantage of this system was that first one home then the other could be classified as their secondary residence and thus be 'claimable for' as regards allowances. By doing this, they realised they could get subsidised furniture and renovation work for each house in turn, at the taxpayers' expense.* In Alistair Darling's case, he appears to have performed this ingenious little 'switcheroo' four times in four years. If only he were half as clever when it came to the economy.

---

* *It's worth mentioning that the Commons authorities tried to make out that they would have been publishing all the information relating to allowances in July 2009 anyway and that, therefore, all the* Telegraph *had done was pre-empt this a bit. That's not quite the whole story: what this statement doesn't make clear is the fact that they were planning to release an edited, much less detailed version. For example, the crucial facts about exactly which of the properties had featured in the claims would not have been included in the July release. Funnily enough, these were precisely the details which allowed the whole practice of 'flipping' to come to light.*

Alistair Darling's flipping house

Minuscule minister Hazel Blears managed to 'flip' her second home three times within one year. Then she sold it, yet simultaneously managed to ensure that it was registered with HM Revenue and Customs as her primary residence, so that no Capital Gains Tax liability was incurred as a result of the sale. When the matter became public knowledge, she said she regretted what she'd done, and hurriedly wrote out a cheque for £13,332 to the Revenue. 'What is really important to me is what people think about this issue, and what they think about me,' she said, neglecting to point out also how important to her keeping her job as an MP was. (She subsequently resigned her Cabinet post in the week of the European and local elections in 2009, and appeared in public wearing a badge reading 'Rocking the boat' – both of which actions she later also said she regretted. Regrets? She's had a few. But then again, too many to mention.)

Blears: On yer flipping bike

And there was further creativity shown in some of the other claims: Peter Mandelson (him again), less than a week after announcing that he was resigning from the Commons, claimed nearly £3,000 for renovation work carried out on his house, a house he then sold (at a profit) after relocating to Brussels to take up his EU job. Conservative MPs were at it too, claiming for horse manure, a housekeeper, pet food, work on the swimming pool or tennis court at their country house here, a chandelier at the manor house there. Tory MP Douglas Hogg repaid the money when he was shown to have submitted a claim for cleaning the moat at his country house. (Owning a moat seems to justify the old saying that 'An Englishman's home is his castle' – though it's not clear whether this castle is the Englishman's primary or secondary home.)

Although, when it comes to taking the biscuit, the House of Commons 'Jammy Dodger' Award goes to former minister and Labour MP Elliot Morley, who claimed £16,000 on a mortgage that he had already paid off. Faced with allegations like this, the police could hardly fail to start taking an interest in the goings on, and resignations duly followed. The Speaker himself, Michael Martin MP, was forced to step down – the first Speaker to have had to do so in 300 years. So well done him.

Some MPs managed to keep themselves above this particular fray. Tory Philip Dunne (Ludlow), Lib Dem David Howarth (Cambridge), Labour's Celia Barlow (Hove) and Martin Salter (Reading West, whose Commons nickname, incidentally is 'Stinky': he used to be a dustman) were notable for being among the relatively few parliamentarians not to be coated by the same extra-large brush of this particularly tarry scandal. How did they manage to avoid it? Well, it turns out their cunning scheme was devilishly simple: despite all having constituencies outside London, and therefore being entitled to claim for a second home under the rules... they, er, didn't. The sneaky bastards.

When the MPs' Expenses story broke, part of the problem for the Conservatives was that these claims reminded voters that Tory MP = massive country house. Obviously, this is not an image David

Cameron, as leader of the party, was entirely comfortable with. So keen are the Conservatives to distance themselves from wealth and finery that they have decided their MPs should begin to give up their outside business interests – particularly the members of the Shadow Cabinet. This ruling affected some more than others, but perhaps the hardest hit was William Hague, the Shadow Foreign Secretary, who was estimated by the *Daily Mail* to have raked in somewhere between £65,000 and £95,000 in just over two months towards the end 2008. And to think there was a time not so long ago when he was forced to muddle along on just his MP's salary and whatever he could grub up from hosting tacky topical panel shows at 9 o'clock on Friday evenings on BBC One.

But let no one be in any doubt – the clampdown on expenses for all MPs was harsh indeed. Michael Martin's last act as Speaker was to agree tough new guidelines with the party leaders. How the hearts of the people were lifted when they learned that draconian new rules drawn up in response to the public's outrage were to be implemented without fear or favour from now on.

Here's a table which sets out clearly just how much the rules governing MPs' allowances have changed as a result of the overhaul of the system announced in June 2009.

ITEM CLAIMED	CLAIMABLE **BEFORE** RULES CHANGED?	CLAIMABLE **AFTER** RULES CHANGED?
Rent	Yes	Yes
Mortgage Interest	Yes	Yes
Hotel Accommodation	Yes	Yes
Insurance	Yes	Yes
Council Tax	Yes	Yes
Gas bills	Yes	Yes
Electricity bills	Yes	Yes
Phone bills	Yes	Yes
Food	Yes	Yes
Duck Island / Moat cleaning	Yes	On the whole, probably best not, old chap.

GOVERNMENT SPENDING AND PUBLIC FINANCES

When the Labour Party came to power in 1997, to reassure a jittery City of London it pledged itself to keeping to the same spending plans as the outgoing Conservative administration. This meant that borrowing had to be maintained at approximately the same level. But they soon realised the potential of an existing scheme: Public-Private Partnerships and Private Finance Initiatives.

Many people are confused by the principles behind PPPs [1 – see below] and PFIs [2], but they needn't be. Put in its simplest form, PPPs [1] are partnerships between the G [3] and one or more PSCs [4] to fund and operate a GS [5] or a PBV [6]. PFIs [2] were seen as a way of encouraging PPPs [1]. In a PFI [2], the PS [7] provides the CI [8] on the strength of a GC [9] to provide an AS [10]. The G [3] may contribute to the PFI [2] by transferring EAs [11]. In projects involving the IS [12], the G [3] may provide a CS [13], for example an OTG [14]. In other cases the G [3] may provide RS [15], which might include TBs [16] or GARs [17]. Often the PSC [4] will form an SPV [18] for the CP [19], and the G [3] may take an ES [20] in the SPV [19]. Not so cocky now, eh, typesetter?

KEY:

PPP [1] – Public-Private Partnership	IS [12] – Infrastructure Sector
PFI [2] – Private Finance Initiative	CS [13] – Capital Subsidy
G [3] – Government	OTG [14] – One-time Grant
PSC [4] – Private Sector Company/Consortium	RS [15] – Revenue Subsidy
GS [5] – Government Service	TB [16] – Tax Break
PBV [6] – Private Business Venture	GAR [17] – Guaranteed Annual Revenue
PS [7] – Private Sector	SPV [18] – Special Purpose Vehicle
CI [8] – Capital Investment	CP [19] – Contracted Period
GC [9] – Government Contract	ES [20] – Equity Share
AS [10] – Agreed Service	
EA [11] – Existing Assets	

And here are some diagrams that explain the relationships more fully:

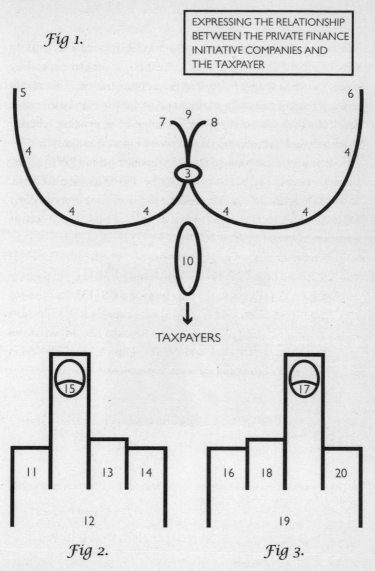

Fig 1.

EXPRESSING THE RELATIONSHIP BETWEEN THE PRIVATE FINANCE INITIATIVE COMPANIES AND THE TAXPAYER

TAXPAYERS

Fig 2.   *Fig 3.*

Now that that's all perfectly clear, please read on.

PFIs have been controversial ever since they first appeared on the political horizon. They had been floating around since 1992, the brainchild of John Major – and let's face it, that should probably have told everyone something about them from the word go. Labour were characteristically vocal in criticising the idea of PFIs at the time, expressing their suspicions that the whole exercise was nothing more than privatisation wearing a different hat. Indeed one senior Labour figure, in his own charmingly Private Fraser-esque way, warned that 'apparent savings now could be countered by the formidable commitment on revenue expenditure in years to come.' Now who might that have been? Step forward Alistair Darling, the current Chancellor of the Exchequer (name and office correct at time of writing). Little did Darling suspect the scale of the 'formidable commitment on revenue expenditure in years to come' for which he and Prime Minister Gordon Brown were to be responsible.

Darling – 'We're all doomed!'

Yet just two months after Labour came to power in 1997, the tone on PFI had changed to such a miraculous degree that the arch-Blairite Health Secretary Alan 'More Time With My Family' Milburn was able to announce: 'When there is a limited amount of public-sector capital available, as there is, it's PFI or bust'. The fact that there might well be a third alternative – PFI *and* bust – didn't seem to

HOW PFIs WORK

The appeal of PFI to any party in government is straightforward. In the old days, if the Government wanted to undertake a big project – like building a hospital – and if it didn't actually have the money, it had to borrow it. Money the Government borrows shows up, quite rightly, as part of the public sector debt in the Government's own 'balance sheet', and has to be taken into account along with all other borrowings when determining how much it is safe to borrow. However, if the financing is undertaken by means of a PFI, the borrowing is technically done not by the Government but by the private company which is in partnership with the Government. Any risk involved in taking on the project is therefore passed to the investors, and in return for taking on this risk they are paid through their contract with the relevant Government department, Health Trust or whatever.

This sneaky bit of accounting meant that governments were able to make the figures for public debt look a lot better than they were, by camouflaging the borrowing that was involved, and making the debt look not like debt at all. Ta da! For Gordon Brown, this aspect of PFIs was particularly important because, as Chancellor for ten years under Tony Blair, he built his reputation by claiming to have a uniquely prudent approach to the public finances. If someone had been smart enough to wangle a pound for every cartoon or political sketch-writer's piece involving Gordon Brown and some weedy reference to a woman called Prudence, he'd have just about enough money to pay off our national debt.

PruDence
(The Squeeze)

HACK
matchstick.com

occur to anyone at the time. And, to be fair, it would take about eleven or twelve years for this particular 'Third Way' to become a realistic possibility.

As Chancellor, Brown's method was to lay down a set of almost impenetrable fiscal rules and tests, which only he fully understood. By appearing to monitor the Treasury's performance and that of the economy against his own rules and tests, he succeeded in convincing nearly everyone that he knew what he was doing, that everything was fine, and that the Government's borrowing levels were both realistic and sustainable, and not just in the good times. Prudence, apparently, was to be his middle name.

POP QUIZ

Q: What actually is Gordon Brown's middle name?
A: Gordon.
Obviously, his name isn't Gordon Gordon Brown – that would be ridiculous. Although some would consider it to be in keeping with the Scottish reputation for parsimony. In fact he was christened James Brown.

James Brown on his first day as PM: 'I feel good (der-ner-ner-ner-ner-ner-ner). I knew that I would now.'

Interestingly, Gordon Brown's father's middle name was Ebenezer. Make of that what you will.

Anyway, as judge, jury, character witness, stenographer and Chancellor, Gordon had it all covered. Anyone coming up against him in the Commons found themselves deluged by a veritable tsunami of statistics and figures, which were quite difficult to argue against because to argue, you need the facts, and Gordon and his Treasury team of wonks (including head wonk Ed Balls) were geniuses at keeping them to themselves. In the beginning were the facts, and the facts were with Gordon. And if Gordon kept telling you that he wasn't breaking the rules that he'd set himself, then he couldn't understand a) how you could possibly doubt him and b) how anything could possibly go wrong.

Blair and Brown wanted to boost levels of investment in schools and hospitals, in line with previous commitments. Brown wasn't about to put up taxes – what are you, crazy? Labour had learned its lesson on that re-election-threatening strategy a long time ago. But nor was Brown about to let the little matter of the money to finance the investment having to come from somewhere spoil the fun. PFI appeared to hold out the promise of a brave new world of 'not-really' borrowing – a way of raising levels of investment without raising public debt and looking like a socialist. As a result, the New Labour administration decided to embrace PFI with the enthusiasm of Alastair Campbell embracing the f-word with 'cynical' journalists. The Labour Party as a whole held its collective nose and kept its collective mouth shut. It was as if they'd never had the slightest reservation about PFI in the first place. Those who tried to point out that there might actually have been something in the original objections to PFI (that, in the long term, undertaking PFI projects would result in the taxpayer having to fork out up to three times as much as they would have had to under a more straightforward, old-fashioned funding scheme) were either just ignored or told they were 'out of touch with modern realities'. PPP, in the form of PFI, was here to stay.

The 'Credit Crunch' and the subsequent worldwide recession have changed the climate for PFI. The drying-up of lending inevitably put the kibosh on the sort of funding upon which PFI projects depend. A spokesman for the PPP Forum told the BBC in 2009: 'Although there is debt available, there is not much of it and the terms are much too expensive ... Because we are having problems raising funding, what we are now looking at is alternative funding structures.' Guess what those 'alternative funding structures' might involve? That's right – somewhere along the line the Government (i.e. the taxpayer) will probably end up having to step in to somehow make up the projected shortfall in funding, which some estimates at the start of 2009 put at about forty per cent of existing and projected PFI projects.

Thanks, pal, but I'm not sure it's going to be enough

PART FIVE

DAILY LIFE IN THE UK

HOUSING

Until the Second Great World Depression, which began in 2008 and which will last until it stops, there had been increasing concern that the price of houses in the UK was getting out of hand. Banks were lending vast sums to people whose ability to pay them back was highly questionable. The era of the 110 per cent mortgage had arrived, and the process of self-certification as regards income became commonplace. As a result, in the years leading up to 2008, the mortgage application procedure for the self-employed went something like this:

Potential house-buyer: 'Hello, I'd like a mortgage to buy a new house please.'

Mortgage lender: 'How much do you want to borrow?'

Potential house-buyer: 'How much will you let me borrow?'

Mortgage lender: 'How much do you earn?'

Potential house-buyer: 'How about if I sign a document stating that I earn exactly enough to allow you to lend me the money to buy a new house?'

Mortgage lender: 'Well, you appear to have thought this application through very carefully, and are obviously just the sort of borrower we're looking to attract. Congratulations – sign here'.

It's ironic that houses suddenly became very much cheaper in the immediate aftermath of the financial crisis, yet no one could buy one because at the same time the banks either collapsed or had the equivalent of a collective nervous breakdown, so mortgage lending dried up almost completely. Luckily, there was a simultaneous expansion of the rented housing sector and many middle-class people suddenly decided to 'go into the property rental business'. Or at least that's what they told people at dinner parties. In reality, what they were doing was renting out the house they'd bought eighteen months earlier at the very top of the market with a massive mortgage calculated on the basis of Josh's past few bonuses, and which had been on the market for nine months already with absolutely no offers at all, and downsizing into rented accommodation simply in order not to be repossessed. Still, 'going into the property rental business' is a rather more concise way of putting it.

MORTGAGE APPLICATIONS

A useful thing to remember when buying a house with a mortgage is that it's important to tell the truth on your mortgage application form. Lenders will ask for details of all the other financial commitments of an applicant; not to reveal significant other borrowings could, under certain circumstances, be construed as criminal. Let's take an example: someone applies for a £150,000 mortgage with a building society, but doesn't happen to declare that they are also being lent a sum in the region of £370,000 by, say, a colleague at work in order to buy the house in question. The consequences could be very serious – if the facts subsequently come to light, the borrower might end up losing his job.

Q: What can you do if you're stuck on a fixed-rate mortgage deal that was agreed at, say, 6% when interest rates fall to below 1%?

A: Nothing at all. Absolutely nothing. Bastards.

Q: How do the banks justify charging as much as 26% interest on credit cards when the bank rate has fallen to below 1%?

A: They don't even try. They just laugh.

Q: Is there any point in trying to buy a house when prices will always be inflated much more than wages; when you will still be paying off your student loan well into your 30s and you will have to start putting money away for a pension if you don't want to be living in a home until you're 65?

A: No.

THE CREDIT CRUNCH

The collapse of the global financial system and the subsequent withdrawal of loans and overdrafts to ordinary people and businesses created widespread misery, not least because everybody from world leaders to newsreaders to know-alls in the pub started using the phrase 'credit crunch', as if they knew what it meant and everyone else 'in the know' was saying it; like one of those supposedly cool phrases such as '24/7', 'don't even go there' and 'heads-up'. In fact, not many people understand the true origins and consequences of the crunch on credit, and none of the respectable media organisations have produced a simple, easy-to-understand guide to the collapse of the global banking system. Until now.

THE COLLAPSE OF THE
GLOBAL BANKING SYSTEM EXPLAINED

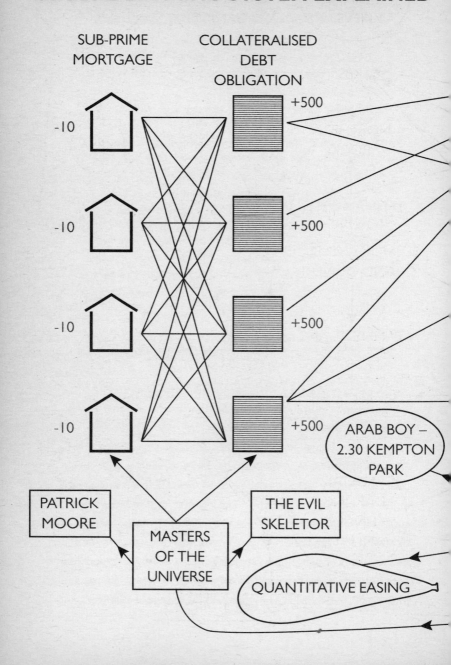

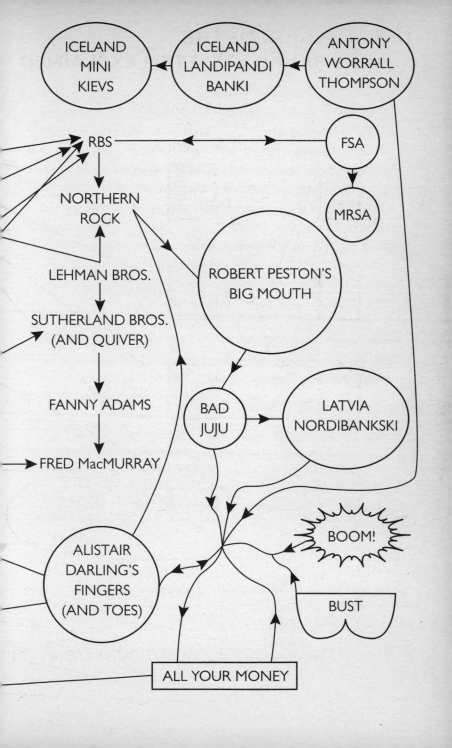

SERVICES IN AND FOR THE HOME

All the utilities (telephone, water, electricity, gas) were once owned by the taxpayer, because they had been 'nationalised'. During the Thatcher era, they were progressively 'privatised', i.e. sold off by the Government to investors through its friends in the City of London, who selflessly made vast profits out of the process. The Conservatives insisted at the time that this sell-off was good for the taxpayer, and they maintain this position today. Stubbornly, however, the taxpayer continues to believe that he or she was totally shafted, and that the money the Government raked in from selling off national assets that weren't really theirs to sell only served to fund the very tax cuts that helped get the Conservative Party re-elected. There's gratitude for you.

Today, a free market in such basic services means individual householders have complete freedom to choose which company they get ripped off by. Indeed, you can switch between companies quickly and easily just by going online. Of course this doesn't mean

It's not possible to switch your water supplier in the UK unless you use more than fifty megalitres a year. That's about twenty-five Olympic swimming pools full of water. Anything less than that and they simply can't be arsed. And to give you an idea of the attitude water companies have towards their customers, here's a quote from a water consumer website:

If you feel that your water company could be doing more to cut wastage, reduce prices or protect the environment, then it's worth considering your own water use by using efficiency measures. This will give you confidence that you are doing your bit.

In other words, fuck off.

that workmen will come and re-lay a pipe to your house – it simply means… well, it means that you could end up paying more than your neighbour for the same gas. Your bill might have a nicer logo on it than theirs, though. So, won't they be really jealous?

Prices of essential supplies such as electricity, water and gas are set by the market, and competition is supposed to ensure that pricing stays competitive. Regulators for each of the industries monitor prices and the performance of suppliers constantly. When they find evidence of anti-competitive activities such as price-fixing, they are entitled to impose fines which can often amount to, ooh, several pounds.

There is some controversy about pricing of energy supplies, but it should be made clear that the pricing code of conduct for the utility companies is robust yet flexible, to allow for market fluctuations. It's certainly flexible enough to ensure that in the event of a rise in wholesale prices (i.e. the price the companies have to pay for their raw materials) the rise is always passed on straight away to the consumer. And it's robust enough to ensure that when the wholesale prices fall again, consumer prices don't budge an inch.

RUBBISH COLLECTION

Collection of household rubbish is the responsibility of the local council. Just as, in the home, it's the responsibility of the man. Many councils have decided that weekly collections are simply unnecessary, and they have been abolished. Some local authorities are thinking of taking this process of rationalisation to its logical conclusion: rubbish collection would be once a year, in order to encourage recycling. In advance of the annual collection, householders would be obliged to sort their recycling alphabetically (from Absinthe bottles down to cartons of Zabaglione), and failure to do so would result in the recycling teams refusing to take it away at all. Houses and flats in these areas must provide themselves with twenty-six 'minnie-wheeliebinnies'™. Alternatively, legislation being considered for after the next election may oblige householders to deliver their rubbish personally to any one of a hundred different recycling centres, from where it can be carefully graded, collected and transported to landfill sites in China.

YOUR LOCAL RECYCLING CENTRE

Taking your rubbish to the local dump (now rebranded as a 'Recycling Centre') used to be a fun, carefree experience. Not any more – it's more like having to sit a GCSE without ever having actually done the course. When you go, you should be prepared to:

a)   have your black plastic bags ripped open and every single item examined intimately

b)   spend at least an hour at the centre, simply trying to figure out which skips relate to which materials, and

c)   endure the heavy sarcasm and withering condescension of the attendants when you finally give up trying to figure it out and decide to just plump for one that looks likely. ('Now then, what have we got here? A juice carton, yes I can see that. So juice cartons go in with the rest of the cardboard, do they madam? No, they don't, because they're only 75 per cent paper, the rest consisting of…? Oh dear, oh dear: 20 per cent plastic, 5 per cent aluminium foil. I thought everyone knew that. Right, off you – whoa, just a minute: does that look like metal to you?')

HEALTH SERVICES

In general, in the UK it's best to try and be ill between the hours of 9 a.m. and 5 p.m. – doctors like to keep regular hours. If you're ill outside these times, there's always NHS Direct, a relatively new service that means you can speak to someone twenty-four hours a day. The chances are, after a lengthy telephone consultation, they'll tell you they can't make a diagnosis over the phone and that you should really make an appointment to see a doctor.

According to published figures, waiting times for operations have been steadily falling. The Government also maintains that the imposition of specific targets within the Health Service (a keynote of New Labour's approach) has been a good thing. Some patient groups dispute that this has improved the service, and say that any reallocation of resources that's based purely around the need to meet specific targets may very well end up distorting priorities and compromising care in the long term. But hey, what do they know?

HOSPITAL-ACQUIRED INFECTIONS – A STRATEGY

A simple course of action to avoid catching MRSA or C. difficile: don't go within fifty miles of a hospital. Luckily, this is a lot easier now than it used to be.

LEISURE ACTIVITIES

Thanks to the financial collapse, many people have a great deal more leisure time than they used to. Surveys show that the UK's favourite leisure activity is shopping. The second favourite is taking things back and having a row with the shop. (Unless, of course, it's Marks and Spencer, but even they have tightened up their procedures recently to try and stop people buying things, wearing them once and then taking them back, which apparently, some people used to do quite a lot. You know who you are.)

In the UK, most cities and larger towns feature a 'Leisure Centre', where people can access facilities such as machines selling chocolate, fizzy pop and crisps, and occasionally a swimming pool or gymnasium. Indeed it is from using facilities like these that many young people get their first valuable taste of the simple enjoyment that comes from having a verruca. In addition, a number of private health club chains have sprung up in recent years, many of them run by the grumpy Scots one off *Dragon's Den* – the one whose catchphrase is 'I'm out.' Or perhaps they all say that. Whatever.

The good news is that, on average, children now spend less of their leisure time slumped in front of the TV than they did a few years ago. The bad news is that this is because they're slumped in front of the computer instead, either keeping in contact with friends through social networking sites, or catching up on BBC Four documentaries downloaded via iPlayer. Although it does mean the internet is running a little slower now than it used to back in the days when the only thing on it was porn. And they call that progress.

TRAVEL AND TRANSPORT

The UK is one of the world's leaders in terms of the cost per mile of rail travel – so well done us. In the past, the Government has provided large subsidies for train-operating companies, enabling them to pay large bonuses over the years to their senior management. This is obviously important, as otherwise the top people in the industry would have to settle for just being paid a hefty salary.

Rail fares are monitored and regulated by the Government, and a formula is applied to enable the train operators to raise them in line with inflation. However, in a time of *de*flation, such as during a world recession for example, when they are prevented from raising the actual fares, train companies have been forced to come up with fresh ideas for extracting money from passengers, the latest one being to get them to pay £5 over and above the normal price of a return ticket just for the right to be able to sit down on one of their trains. (If you want a cup of tea and a Kit-Kat, it's an extra £15). It will be interesting to watch their PR departments trying to spin that one.

On the roads, 'road-pricing' has been in the offing for a number of years. Hailed as a success, the UK's first pay-as-you-go stretch of motorway opened in 2003, enabling motorists to avoid Birmingham completely. It's not necessarily a reliable indicator, though: who in their right mind wouldn't want to do that? 2003 also saw the introduction of the London Congestion Charge – effectively a tax levied on vehicles entering the capital. The economic impact of the scheme is clear: if you get your car out and drive into the centre of London, by the time you've paid the Congestion Charge on top of car tax, road tax, car-insurance tax, fuel tax and Value Added Tax, you'll have paid more UK tax in one day than Roman Abramovich has since he moved here.

EMPLOYMENT

In the UK, there are Government-run offices that try to help people without work to find it. In the old days, they used to be called 'Labour Exchanges' – the implication being that there was in fact no lack of jobs, it was just that some people might like to exchange their job for someone else's. Nowadays, they are called 'Jobcentres' – which was obviously intended to sound like an upbeat, airy place with muzak and chit-chat, although in the middle of a global recession it has a definite 'newspeak' undertone.

In the past, they were also simply referred to as the 'Dole Office', because 'the Dole' was what you received from the state when you were unemployed. Nowadays, the unemployed receive the much more dynamic-sounding 'Jobseeker's Allowance'. (See? Spin works.) Although it's probably a good thing that this name wasn't brought in during the 1980s, because it would have undoubtedly affected the quality of slogans chanted by striking miners.

'Coal, not Jobseeker's Allowance'
doesn't have quite the same ring to it

It's interesting that the Government should have decided to refer to what was previously known as a 'benefit' ('Unemployment Benefit') as an 'Allowance' instead. During the initial stages of the furore that erupted in 2009 over how much taxpayers' money MPs had been claiming (for paying their mortgages, buying furniture, cleaning moats and employing housekeepers, etc.; see above), one of the weedy defences they put forward was that they were *allowances*, not expenses. And precisely because they *were* allowances, they believed it was basically an entitlement, and therefore they assumed they didn't actually have to justify them in any way.

There's a rather more complicated procedure to endure if you're claiming 'Jobseeker's Allowance' (to enable you to, say, feed your family after you've lost your job). It's far more painstaking than the one for claiming 'Moat-Cleaner's Allowance', for example. So spare a thought for the poor chiselling bastards who were dumped over the 'expenses' row, dealing with the rather more demanding paperwork that claiming 'Jobseeker's Allowance' entails.

THE WORKING ENVIRONMENT

In Britain, the workplace is a very different environment today from how it was in the past. Large, open-plan, glass-walled offices provide excellent opportunities for the sort of people who like to know everything about their co-workers to indulge their hobby. Coincidentally, these are very often the same people who seem to feel the need to share all the minutiae of their own life with

---

What you can expect at work:

1. Access to a kettle which has never been de-scaled.
2. Access to a water-cooler, otherwise how else do you find out who's shagging whom this week?
3. Photographs of children stuck to computers (the photographs, obviously, not the children).
4. A health and safety person who'll visit once every two years or so, stare at you for a bit while you awkwardly try and get on with some work, then say things like 'Hmm – do you always sit slightly twisted like that?' And every time they come round they'll make a point of recommending that you take a break from your computer screen every twenty minutes or so. And they'll manage to do this with such a straight face it's almost as if they believe this is a realistic suggestion.
5. Access to a toilet which has inevitably been befouled by the previous user. As you leave the toilet, you will pass a colleague as they enter the same cubicle. This is guaranteed to happen with the same colleague at least twice. From this point on they will always politely decline your offer of a cup of tea when you're doing a round. Which, at least, is something.

---

everyone else too. In a modern office, it is important to be seen to go along with this – on no account should you attempt to keep any of the details of your private life to yourself. Doing so will result in your being labelled 'secretive', 'insular', 'uncooperative', 'unfriendly', 'unapproachable', 'difficult', 'grumpy' or, worst of all in HR speak, 'not a team player'.

It is important to remember that in offices in this country, whilst it remains perfectly OK for a man to slope off early because the football team he supports is playing yet another match against Dynamo Bratislava in the Benski Bank AG Euro-League or whatever, in the workplace of today it is never permissible for a man to arrange to go home a bit early because he wants to spend some time with his children.

It is also vital to bear in mind that when a football fan receives a text message telling him that the draw has just taken place for some competition or other, it is regarded as completely acceptable for him to stop concentrating on what he's doing (breaking off in mid-sentence if necessary) and either bring to an abrupt end or at least entirely disrupt any meeting he might be in, however important, in order to send and/or receive in his turn anything up to twenty urgent text messages to and/or from friends saying things like 'hav u heard the draw i dont belieeeeeeve it liverpool again' or alternatively 'hahaha you gonna get stuffed bad luck mate roflmao'.

CHILDCARE AND CHILDREN AT WORK
In the UK, employers are increasingly aware of the demands made by family life on mothers of small children. So they employ men instead.

EQUAL RIGHTS AND DISCRIMINATION
The UK has come a long way: now the only group regularly discriminated against are ginger people. Many people still think it's acceptable to be rude about them. No one knows why.

Gingers: Simply mutants

SALARIES

It is important to be aware that working for just a salary has come to be regarded as ridiculously old-fashioned in the UK. For years, we have been assured that people (or 'top people' at least) need 'incentivising'. It used to be the case, of course, that a) getting paid for doing a job, b) actually *wanting* to do it well, and c) *not* wanting to get sacked were incentive enough, but no longer. Now it seems that more or less everybody is paid a bonus on top of their salary. The relationship between size of bonus and company performance or personal achievement often seems unclear, however. Whilst it is true that Sir Fred Goodwin's personal achievement was remarkable, the thing that he personally achieved was the bankrupting of RBS, the bank he was head of. That his reward for breaking the bank should have been so staggeringly large proved to be a source of complete bafflement to many people. Not to say absolute blind, frothy-mouthed, purple-faced fury. Especially in the case of RBS shareholders themselves.

KNOWING THE LAW

Every person in the UK has the right to equal treatment under the law. This means that the law applies in the same way to everyone, and that everyone, regardless of who they are or where they come from, can expect equal treatment by the authorities and the police. There are some exemptions from this general principle, of course – Brazilians travelling on the London Underground, or newspaper sellers caught up in demonstrations whilst making their way home.

When it comes to lawyers, the rule of thumb is pretty much the same as when visiting some of those shops in and around Bond Street: if you have to ask how much it costs, you probably can't afford it. However, people who simply cannot afford the fees that lawyers

'Celebrities' are able to take advantage of certain procedures not available to ordinary people – on occasion, when a famous person is stopped for speeding, the police will often choose to deal with the case using a 'fast-track' system designed to save the courts time. Under this system, the famous person is obliged to sign their name several times on several different pieces of paper, then have their photograph taken at the roadside standing with their arm round one of the officers, preferably smiling and doing the 'thumbs-up' sign, while a colleague takes a photograph of the incident using a mobile phone. The procedure is repeated, the number of repetitions being equal to the number of police officers with camera-phones at the scene. The resulting documentary evidence is then circulated widely both within that particular force and to selected members of other forces, for information purposes.

charge (somewhere in the region of ninety-nine per cent of the population) can apply for legal aid. The system is designed in such a way as to allow many different categories of claimant to be granted aid. In the past, not just the sons of crooked newspaper magnates who fell off yachts in the Mediterranean but also extremist religious preachers who had publicly pledged themselves to the overthrow of this country's entire system of government (including, one assumes, its legal aid system) have successfully claimed taxpayers' money to help fight their court cases.

REPORTING A CRIME

Dialling 999 or 112 (112? – who knew?) in the event of an emergency gives access to the emergency services – fire, police, ambulance and coastguard. Despite campaigns over the years, it is still the case that the provision of coastguard services is extremely patchy in the UK. It remains a scandal that there are plenty of coastguard stations to provide cover for one of England's smallest counties, the Isle of Wight, yet not a single coastguard is assigned to the Birmingham area. Astonishingly, successive governments have failed to get to grips with this blatant inequality. Until they do, you should only ask for the coastguard service if the incident is taking place at or near the coast.

If the situation is NOT an emergency, you can telephone your local police station – and the adjective 'local' is here used in possibly its loosest sense. If you don't know the number of your local police station, you can find the address and telephone number in the phone book. If you can find the phone book. If you can't find it, you could try putting 'Police' into Google. Then, after you've got distracted by scrolling through Sting's biography (he can do tantric sex, apparently) and several pages of quite pricey sunglasses as modelled by David Beckham, the emergency will probably have gone away all by itself.

Some minor crimes can also be reported online – the advantages of this from the police's point of view are a) they don't have to actually speak to members of the public in person at any point, and b) they can always say they never got it because the server was down that day. However, if the report you wish to make happens to involve the purchase of Viagra at discount prices, or contains news of some bloke in Nigeria who's mysteriously come into a fortune, but who in order to claim it needs a relatively small sum of money sending urgently (by Western Union only please), it is more than likely to be returned by the police's spam filter. Consequently, any incidents of this type are probably best reported in the usual manner.

THE COURTS

Broadly speaking, there are two types of court case – civil and criminal. The burden of proof is different in both: in a civil case, it is generally described as being 'on the balance of probabilities', whereas in criminal cases it is 'beyond reasonable doubt' (except in the OJ Simpson trial, where the bar appeared to have been set considerably higher than that). Courts are presided over by judges, who don't always get a good press. The popular image of senior High Court judges is that of a dusty, crusty, old-fashioned, remote, aloof, unsympathetic elite who delight in displaying their complete ignorance of the realities of everyday life for many of the people who appear before them. However, this stereotype is less than accurate: many judges are much worse than that.

THE HUMAN RIGHTS ACT

The principles of the European Convention on Human Rights were enshrined in British Law in the Human Rights Act of 1998. Amongst the rights listed by the Home Office, for example, are the following three:

1. 'Prohibition of torture – no one should be tortured or punished or treated in an inhuman or degrading way.'

Excellent. Bear in mind that this may not apply if you're being interrogated by our allies the Americans, and either waterboarded on the spot or flown to a different country for interrogation, as the British Government apparently reserves the right to either just turn a blind eye or sometimes actively collude to facilitate your 'extraordinary rendition'. (Not to be confused with 'extraordinary rendering' which is basically 'pebbledash'.)

2. 'The right to Liberty and Security – everyone has the right not to be detained or have their liberty taken away, unless it is within the law and the correct legal procedures are followed.'

Be aware that the Government reserves the right to keep on trying to get legislation through to extend the period the police are able to hold suspects without charge. The initial proposal, in the wake of the London bombings, was for an extension to 90 days; it was defeated in the Commons so they settled for 28, but kept making noises about increasing it to 42. In 2008, however, the President of the Association of Chief Police Officers went even further, calling for it to be possible to hold suspects indefinitely. A lot of valuable parliamentary time is wasted on the argument over 'numbers of days', when the whole problem could easily be sorted out by Death Squads.

3. 'The right to freedom of assembly and association – everyone has the right to get together with other people in a peaceful way.'

This may not apply if, say, you're trying to protest peacefully by reading out the names of British soldiers killed in Iraq at the Cenotaph in Whitehall. In which case you'll probably be arrested under the provisions of the Serious Organised Crimes and Police Act of 2005.

MODERN BRITAIN – WHERE ARE WE NOW?

As this book goes to print, there are a number of possible scenarios for what may have happened, politically speaking, by the time it actually hits the shelves. Some of them are listed below and have been run past the experts at a-major-high-street-betting-chain in order to give some sort of perspective on how likely (or not) they are to have come to pass in the intervening months. The odds they quoted are listed below so, however bad things have got, readers can at least cheer themselves up with the thought of how much they could have won or lost had events panned out other than they did. Here are the scenarios they were asked to quote odds for:

Gordon Brown is still Prime Minister, the Cabinet reshuffle of June 2009 did, in the end, enable him to re-establish his authority with the Cabinet, with backbenchers, with the Labour Party and with the country at large. **Odds: EVENS**

Gordon Brown is still Prime Minister, but even those members of the Cabinet who supported him after the June reshuffle are beginning to look at the floor and clear their throats audibly whenever he speaks, then sidle away as if they've suddenly remembered they've left the gas on. Despite his ever more frequent and desperate gurning appearances on 'YouTube', the country at large is sick to death of the sight of him. **Odds: 4/1 ON**

Gordon Brown is no longer Prime Minister, and look who is: it's the grand old survivor Jack Straw, who, when the dust settled, somehow emerged as a sort of 'caretaker PM' (although, funnily enough, that's not quite how Jack sees it). As a result, the long-suffering country is stuck with yet another Prime Minister chosen not openly by the electorate, but behind closed doors by members of the Labour Party. (After Thatcher was chucked out, even the Tories only had the gall to pull that stunt once.) Odds: 33/1	Gordon Brown is no longer Prime Minister, but, rather embarrassingly, it's quite hard to tell who is. It would appear to be someone called Ed – or is it David? Or Alan. Or (an outside bet, this) James. Since they all look and sound much the same, nobody's really all that bothered about which one of them it is, and if they're honest none of them actually wanted the job at this particular juncture, since they all know that soon the party won't be worth leading anyway. Odds: 2/1
Gordon Brown is no longer Prime Minister. Tony Blair is. Odds: EVENS	Gordon Brown is no longer Prime Minister. David Cameron is. Odds: 100/30
Gordon Brown is no longer Prime Minister. Boris Johnson is. Odds: NO ODDS GIVEN	Gordon Brown is no longer Prime Minister – Peter Mandelson is. Desperate times call for desperate measures, and let's face it that's about as desperate as measures get. As a member of the Upper House, he's not allowed into the House of Commons, so Prime Minister's Questions is now held in the Dome. Odds: 9/4

Leaving aside for the moment the ticklish issue of who happens to be in Number 10 when this book comes out, what can be said more generally about the state of the UK at the end of the first decade of the new millennium? What should we be worried about as the century gets under way? The following issues have presented themselves during the course of the writing of this book, and are peeping up over an otherwise blue and cloudless horizon.

Obviously, the rock-bottom nature of the esteem in which MPs are held is a hugely significant development – not that they were ever held up as paragons of virtue exactly. But perhaps the public's reaction to the allowances scandal can be summed up by a letter to the *Daily Telegraph*: when the MP Julie Kirkbride (after pressure from her constituents over her claims) announced that she had decided to stand down at the next election, a correspondent helpfully suggested that since she had already been a journalist before becoming an MP, perhaps she might now like to try her hand at estate agency. Public esteem can surely go no lower.

The turn-out at the most recent EU elections also fell to an historic low at around thirty-five per cent. At this point it's quite hard to see how public trust in the UK's politicians and the UK's political system can be restored after the allowances affair. Everyone seems agreed that Parliament is overdue for a clean-out. Yet the people who put themselves forward as alternative MPs in the wake of the affair turned out to be the likes of David 'Used-To-Be-In-Dollar' Van Day.

If the answer is David Van Day, what was the question?

The widespread disillusionment with mainstream politics would appear to have resulted in the resurgence of some of the more extreme parties, namely nationalist parties such as the BNP, who won two council seats in 2009, and whose leader was elected as an MEP. It's funny how the words 'resurgence' and 'nationalist parties' somehow never sit altogether comfortably in the same sentence, particularly for anyone who studied the 1930s in any detail at school. (Still, the teaching of that sort of old-fashioned history is no doubt in line to be phased out, in favour of lessons devoted to topics such as 'How to get the most out of Twitter'.)

And it's not just the Commons, of course – the half-arsedly reformed House of Lords has had its own scandals recently, resulting in suspensions for the first time in centuries. Previously, the Lords was frequently described as being 'stuck in a time-warp', but many believe that was preferable to the sort of credibility limbo it now finds itself in, still with a clingy hereditary rump but largely stacked with mates (albeit perhaps mostly now former mates) of Tony and Gordon. For example, Glenys Kinnock may be a nice person, who knows, and it's possible she may actually know a bit about her new brief. But the fact remains that she leapfrogged into the position of Minister for Europe after being bounced directly into the Lords by Gordon Brown as part of his last-ditch reshuffle. The implication of her rather hasty appointment is clear: there are 640-odd people in the Commons, duly elected by their constituents to represent them, yet NONE of them was apparently capable of doing the job. That doesn't say much about the state of the Commons. Or rather, it actually says quite a lot.

'We're offering you the job, Glenys, because we can't think of anyone better.'

Meanwhile, if the Lisbon Treaty or its successor eventually comes to be ratified in some form or other, there'll be a further transference of power away from Westminster towards Brussels. The Scottish Parliament and the Welsh Assembly have been eyeing up more powers for a while now. Tomorrow's UK Government revenues (in other words, our future taxes) have already been pledged to help shore up the teetering financial structures of yesterday, in an attempt to stave off the total collapse of the system in the face of a full-blown, super-sized, worldwide stinkeroony of a recession. The UK's own credit-worthiness is threatened – we are told that the country's international credit rating is constantly under review and faces being downgraded as the national debt swallows up an ever greater proportion of the country's GDP, and as 'Quantitative Easing' further undermines faith in the currency. And if people thought the pensions crisis was bad before, the stock-market slump and the associated drop in dividends has meant significantly lower returns for the very funds upon which most people's pensions depend.

Then there's the fact that the relaxation of licensing laws only means the average 18–35-year-old's five-evenings-a-week binge-drinking sessions can now start and finish later. And the proliferation of CCTV cameras, ostensibly to control the resulting anti-social behaviour, has gone hand in hand with the expansion of databases of varying degrees of concern to civil liberties campaigners. At the same time, there's been an increasing use of anti-terror legislation for purposes for which it was never intended. The commitment of British troops in Afghanistan looks likely to be a virtually open-ended one. The rise of radical fundamentalism within the UK together with the revelation of the extent of the country's links with destabilising elements in nuclear-ready Pakistan threaten to undermine the security of both the region and the whole world. Oh, and let's not forget swine flu is waiting in the wings.

Still, on the plus side, at least *Big Brother* is still going. And *The Apprentice* (as long as Lord Siralan's governmental commitments don't get in the way too much). What else? Oh yes – the United Kingdom entry finished in the top five in the Eurovision Song Contest, despite Andrew Lloyd Webber's appearance.

So it's not all bad, then. Welcome to Modern Britain.

EDITOR'S NOTE

The bulk of this book was written in May/June 2009. At that stage, nobody could have imagined the situation arising where Gordon Brown would have to be formally relieved of the Premiership following his increasingly erratic behaviour. Because it occurred at a photo-call, and there were more than a hundred of the world's top news photographers in attendance, the particular incident that triggered his departure was very well documented, so there's no need to go into it any further here. Happily, Angela Merkel was eventually persuaded not to press charges. And who would have predicted that one of the indirect beneficiaries would have been the BBC's Political Editor, Nick Robinson, who went on to win a major international journalistic award for his final dramatic interview with Gordon Brown, just as he was being carried out of Number 10 for the last time. (Although the interview itself was a curious one, consisting as it did of the following mysterious phrases muttered over and over again like a mantra: 'Let's make a deal, he said. I'll have first crack at it, then I'll hand over to you, he said. I won't land you in it, he said. You can trust me, Gordon, he said.')

And who could possibly have foreseen that, having seized power in a swift, well-planned and thankfully bloodless coup with the help of a crack contingent of Gurkhas, Prime Minister Lumley would subsequently agree to enter into a formal coalition with the newly formed That's Life Party, in a deal which saw Esther Rantzen take charge of the renamed Department of Fisheries and Funny-Shaped Food. A few months really is a long time in politics.

'Ayo Lumley!'

CONCLUSION
BY PAUL MERTON

Well that was funny, wasn't it? I'm sorry, I drifted off half-way through but I'm sure the rest of you had the time of your lives. And may God have mercy on your souls.

There seems to be a bit of space left, so although it's already on the cover of this book, it's worth re-stating that the series score of 'Have I Got News For You' is Paul 27, Ian 3.

GLOSSARY

This glossary is designed to help anyone new to the English language to understand the meanings of key words and key expressions whose multifarious linguistic functionalities might otherwise remain obfuscated.

Aardvark – Pig-like creature with just two purposes in life – to eat ants and to start dictionaries/ glossaries.

Abusive – Correct mode of behaviour to adopt when telephoned with an offer of a free holiday.

Accountant – Person hired by MPs to ensure they are paying the correct amount of tax, the expense of which will then make headlines in the *Daily Telegraph*, a national newspaper owned by the Barclay brothers, who live in a castle in the Channel Islands in order to avoid paying tax, on the advice of their accountant.

Adultery – See *Johnson, Boris*.

Afford – Have enough money to pay for something. As in: 'So long as he doesn't mind losing matches, Manchester City can afford him.'

Birth Rate – Statistical record of the number of babies born in a country, to help regulate supply to Angelina Jolie and Madonna.

Bishop – Senior priest in the Christian religion. Can only move diagonally.

Boom – See *Bust*.

Building Society – A society that, whatever you may like to think, owns 'your' building.

Bust – Generally associated with financial disaster or, in the case of Katie Price, financial reward. For 'Boom-Bust Cycle', see *Boom*.

By-election – Fleeting moment in the political calendar when a non-descript town in the Midlands is suddenly called 'pivotal' by Nick Robinson.

Cable Company – The only kind of company Jacqui Smith's husband could turn to, one bleak lonely evening.

Charity – Pernicious employer of irritating bastards with clipboards on the streets.

Chieftan – (1) Ruler or leader of a clan in Scotland (antiquated). (2) British army tank (antiquated).

Childminder – Person who looks after your child while you go out to earn just enough money to pay them.

Commemorate – (1) To remember an important person or event with fondness and respect. (2) *Of television* To schedule a whole evening of lazy programming on the flimsy pretext of an anniversary.

Commonwealth of Nations – Contemporary name for the British Empire, to make everyone feel rather better about themselves.

Compensation – Something you can sue absolutely anyone to obtain, except a lawyer.

Concentrate – Word in very small letters on most cartons of FRESH JUICE.

Consumer Society – Weight Watchers.

D-Day – Handy spelling rule.

Destitute – Male prostitute prepared to impersonate Des Lynam. (BBC Books's lawyers have asked us to point out that this is just a joke. Well, we had to include at least *one*.)

Devolution – Opposite of evolution. Popular in Scotland and Wales.

Dioxyribonucleic Acid – Complex molecule containing genetic code. Dioxyribonucleic acid is easily remembered by the following mnemonic – 'Dumb Idiot On Xylophone Yells Raucous Insults Believing Obnoxious Nutters Undermine Chemistry Laboratory Engineers Investigating Chemical Acid Called Incidentally Dioxyribonucleic'. Sometimes obliquely referred to as DNA.

Direct Debit – A painless way of spending money without realising it, until they come to take your children.

Diss – Town in Norfolk, frequently referred to by Los Angeles rappers.

Earth – TV studio owned by David Attenborough.

Ecstasy – Ironically named drug that can lead to misery. (See also *Happy Hour, Smile TV*.)

Endangered Species – Creatures close to extinction, e.g. giant pandas, blue whales, intelligent newsreaders.

Energy – Topic at the heart of the biggest question facing twenty-first-century humankind: 'Are you happy with your energy supplier?'

Express, Daily – Paper which clings to the absurd belief that its readers are only interested in Princess Diana and property prices. And is right.

Euro – Pound, more or less.

Eurovision Song Contest – One of those things everyone knows should be stopped but, at the same time, no one quite cares enough to stop it. See **Poverty, global**.

F-word – What the Germans said on D-Day.

Facebook – Social networking site, essential for planning nights out, parties, murders, etc.

Film Noir – Utterly pointless phase of early cinema, before the invention of Film Noir et Blanc.

Fox, Urban – City dwelling litter-bin inspector, with a second home in the country.

France – The reason why huge gangs of Neolithic Britons dug the English Channel.

Franz Ferdinand – Archduke and bandleader. Biggest hit, 1914, 'Take Me Out'.

Freudian Slip – A big throbbing oral cock-up.

G-spot – Place well worth finding while enjoying an F-word.

Glossary – Meaningless list of meanings; a book filler. 'The last refuge of the scoundrel' (Dr Johnson). 'What about patriotism?' (James Boswell). 'OK then, second-last' (Dr Johnson).

God – Mysterious entity whose existence is firmly believed in by Tony Blair. See *Iraq's Weapons of Mass Destruction*.

Grass – Cannabis. Same as Marijuana.

Grass – Marijuana. Same as Cannabis.

Grass – Weed. Another name for Marijuana. And Cannabis. Not to be confused with Weed.

Grass – Grass that isn't Weed. The bits of green that you should leave in the lawn, whilst plucking out any Weed (see *Grass — Weed*).

Guardian, The – Liberal newspaper that used to be ridiculed for its misprints, although now it's gone computerised, that simply doesn't hoppen.

Hard Shoulder – Lane on side of motorway, for exclusive use of emergency services, breakdown vehicles and confused pensioners on buggies.

High Definition – *adj.* Extending upwards; situated far above ground; not low.

Hospitality, Corporate – Bizarre practice of attempting to gain favour with business contacts by obliging them to attend a sports event which they quite obviously have no interest in watching.

Imam Mia – Musical about Muslim cleric set to ABBA tunes. Closed down before first night.

Insurance – Financial policy that successfully reduces stress, until you attempt to make a claim.

Iran – Same as Iraq.

Iraq – Not to be confused with Iran.

Iraq's Weapons of Mass Destruction – See *Iran*.

January – Hottest month of British summer, 2019.

Jihad – Surprising motive of the killer in Agatha Christie's *Murder at the Vicarage*.

Johnson, Boris – Mayor of London (sic).

King of Pop – Mysterious title briefly bestowed by the tabloids on Michael Jackson after his death, before reverting to the more commonly accepted 'Wacko Jacko'.

Korea, North – Country run by a madman with Weapons of Mass Destruction. Best not invaded.

Kyle, Jeremy – British Prime Minister, 2015–2016.

Llanfairpwllgwyngyllgogerychwyrndrobwllllantysiliogogogoch – (1) Longest town name in the world. (2) Noise Charlotte Church makes when vomiting.

Mail, Daily – See *Political Correctness* and *Red Mist*.

Microwave – Small and insincere gesture of recognition towards complete strangers, made by any politician stepping out of a people carrier.

Minimum Wage – Maximum wage paid by fast-food outlets.

Motorway – Road specially designed to accommodate three lanes of stationary traffic.

Murray Mint – Hefty wodge of cash donated to Britain's top tennis player by the taxpayer for wearing a Royal Bank of Scotland logo on his shirt.

Murray Mount – What Britain's top tennis player does in bed.

Needle, Discarded – Dangerous detritus left behind by drugs users, often found in haystacks.

Neighbourhood Watch – The future of modern policing. Attempt to crack down on rampant crime by sticking little signs on lamp posts – though China still plumps for the death penalty.

Notting Hill Carnival – Joyous street festival held to celebrate the annual theft of David Cameron's bicycle.

Nutritional Value – Meaningless statement on crisp packet.

Orwell, George – Inspirational inventor of TV formats, incl. *Big Brother*, *Room 101*, *Countdown*, etc.

Parkinson's Law – They don't make chat-shows like they used to.

Poet Laureate – Job title which it's oddly hard to find a rhyme for.

Political Correctness – Thing that has gone mad. If we're allowed to say that.

Poverty, Global – See *Eurovision Song Contest*.

Preacher of Hate – Any cleric with an eyepatch or hook. Or the Archbishop of Canterbury on a really bad day.

Q – Under-appreciated genius behind the invention of secret gadgets, fast cars and lethal weapons for James Bond. And the talking bottle-opener.

Quadbike – Preferred means of transport for Oxford don.

Queen Elizabeth II – Creator of 'architecturally abhorrent' glass ceiling for Prince Charles.

Rabid – see *Fox* or *Preacher of Hate*.

Renewables – Any programme on Dave.

Road Rage – Entirely natural psychological consequence of the gap between car adverts and reality.

Sat-Nav – See Destination.

Seventy – Maximum speed limit on Britain's roads. Minimum age of Glastonbury headline act.

Shakespeare, William – A national treasure. The Alan Bennett of his age.

Skunk – Black and white animal of American origin, which gives off a pungent odour when smoked.

Sky Dish – In-flight meal.

Smoothie – What Peter Mandelson sees in the mirror.

Smoothie, Orange – What Dale Winton sees in the mirror.

Swine Flu – What that unhealthy person sniffing right next to you on the train has definitely got.

Talent – What Britain has not got.

Television, Reality – Unreality.

Traffic Warden – Valuable member of society, whose duty is to ensure that the traffic regulations are observed by one and all in an equitable manner which facilitates the harmonious use of public thoroughfares.

Not.

I'd only stopped to pop into the bloody newsagents.

Eighty quid!

Trident – British nuclear weapons programme and key part of the nation's defence strategy. Named after a three-pronged metal spear, which would be just as effective and considerably cheaper.

Twitter – Global communications phenomenon. It was Twitter that enabled a worldwide audience to bypass the censors and find out for themselves the precise moment, during Iran's suppression of post-election demonstrators, that Stephen Fry had started picking his nose.

Uni – What students call that tricky thing with too many syllables in it.

United Kingdom – Disunited region ruled by Queen.

Untenable – Position of any Government minister at any time.

Virgin – What Richard Branson's mother should have remained.

Wire, The – US TV drama with a cult following, set in a cheese shop.

X-Factor – Ancient Roman sun cream.

X-ray – Form of spectacles for seeing through clothing. No other practical use.

Y-i-player – Device for watching online repeats of any show featuring Ant and Dec.

YouTube – Personalised designer enema. Used once, with obvious discomfort, by Gordon Brown.

Zebra Crossing – Pedestrianised strip of road useful for UK glossaries in need of something beginning with 'z'.

Zebu – Humped domestic ox, commonly found in Asia, but not in the United Kingdom.

PICTURE CREDITS

p9: Bruno Vincent/Getty Images; p10 *top*: Paul Merton; p10 *bottom*: Dan Kitwood/Getty Images; p17: Disney; p18 *left*: Jeff J Mitchell/ Getty Images; p18 *right*: Hulton Archive/Getty Images; p19 *top*: Antony Jones/UK Press/Press Association Images; p19 *bottom*: Sol Neelman/ Corbis; p20: Chris Jackson/Getty Images; p25 *top*: Barnabas Kindersley/ Getty Images; p25 *bottom*: Eising/Getty Images; p28: Hulton Archive/ Getty Images; p31: Jon Hicks/Corbis; p33: Hampshire County Council; p34 and p162: Plane Stupid/PA Wire; p36 *top*: Miguel Vidal/Reuters/ Corbis; p36 *bottom*: Dave Hogan/Getty Images; p38 *top left* and *right*: David McKee/Rollo Rights Ltd; p38 *bottom*: Hilary Hayton; p39: Influx Productions/Getty Images; p41: Mark Wilson/Getty Images; p43: Tibor Bognar/Corbis; p45 *top*: Joshua Lott /Reuters/Corbis; p45 *bottom*: akg-images /British Library; p48 *left*: workshop of Sir Anthony van Dyck/The Bridgeman Art Library/Getty Images; p48 *right*: (original without beard) Dan Tuffs/Getty Images; p49: Hulton Archive/Getty Images; p54 *top* and *middle*: Hulton Archive/Getty Images; p54 *bottom*: Time & Life Pictures/ Getty Images; p55: Everett Collection/Rex Features; p56: Popperfoto/ Getty Images; p60: Bettmann/Corbis; p61: Bundesarchiv/ Bild 146-1970-052-24; p68: Zak Hussein/Press Association Images; p71: Chris Jackson/Getty Images; p75: Angelo Hornak/Corbis; p77: Hulton Archive/ Getty Images; p78: Mark Wieland/Getty Images; p81 clockwise from *top left*: Jacob Andrzejczak/Getty Images, Chris Jackson/Getty Images, Jacob Andrzejczak/Getty Images, Scott Barbour/Getty Images, John M. Heller/Getty Images, John M. Heller/Getty Images; p81 *bottom*: Reuters/ Dylan Martinez; p86 *left*: The Open University; p86 *right*: Open Mike Productions; p90: Jeff Overs/BBC; p96 *top*: BWAC Images/Alamy; p96 *bottom*: Rex Features; p97: Rosie Greenway/Getty Images; p110: Political Pictures; p114 *left*: AFP/Getty Images; p114 *right*: Paul Smith/EMPICS Entertainment; p116 *left*: Chris Jackson/Getty Images; p116 *right*: AFP/ Getty Images; p118: Hulton Archive/Getty Images; p120: Philippe Desmazes/AFP/Getty Images; p120 *bottom*: Scott Barbour/Getty Images; p131: Phil Noble/Reuters/Corbis; p132: Felipe Trueba/epa/Corbis; p134: Hulton Archive/Getty Images; p135: AP Photo/B.K. Bangash; p136: Matt Lamy; p137: Paul Barker/AFP/Getty Images; p149 *top*: Alan Simpson; p149 *bottom*: Paul Cousans; p154: Shaun Curry/AFP/Getty Images; p155: Matt Buck; p156: Peter Macdiarmid/Getty Images; p158: Chris Ratcliffe/ Rex Features; p172: Rob Taggart/Bride Lane Library/Popperfoto/Getty Images; p175 Sebastian Willnow/AFP/Getty Images; p183: Roy Catherall/ PA Images; p184: Press Association Images; p187: David Crump/WPA Pool/Getty Images.